P9-CRO-771

The Festive Bread Book

by Kathy Cutler

BARRON'S

Barron's

Woodbury, New York • London • Toronto • Sydney

© Copyright 1982 by Barron's Educational Series, Inc.

All rights reserved.
No part of this book may be reproduced in any form, by photostat, microfilm, xerography, or any other means, or incorporated into any information retrieval system, electronic or mechanical, without the written permission of the copyright owner.

All inquiries should be addressed to:
Barron's Educational Series, Inc.
113 Crossways Park Drive
Woodbury, New York 11797

Library of Congress Catalog Card No. 82-13779
International Standard Book No. 0-8120-5453-9

Library of Congress Cataloging in Publication Data

Cutler, Kathy.
 The festive bread book.

 Bibliography: p. 217
 Includes index.
 1. Bread. I. Title.
TX769.C87 1982   641.8'15   82-13779
ISBN 0-8120-5453-9

Credits:

Photography:
 Bill Helms, color photographs
 France Benko, stylist
 Andrea Swenson, food stylist

Jacket and cover design: Milton Glaser, Inc.

Book design: Milton Glaser, Inc.

PRINTED IN THE UNITED STATES OF AMERICA
4 5 6   410   9 8 7 6 5 4

To my husband, Charles
whose encouragement and help
made this book a reality

Contents

Introduction

Holidays are a golden time for anyone who bakes bread. They provide an ideal opportunity to prepare and serve stollen, hoska, hot cross buns, panettone, St. Basil's bread, and many other festive breads that are less well known. These delicacies add joy to already happy occasions, while remaining a treat at any time.

Yet surprisingly little has been published on festive breads in their own right. I became aware of this lack while teaching bread courses at a number of places in Connecticut. Students, as always, took great pleasure in making festive breads, but neither they nor I were able to find a complete overview of this subject.

So I started to compile my own hoard of recipes from family, friends, students, and old books—and I became so intrigued that I've been collecting holiday bread recipes ever since. The recipes in this book cover 17 specific holidays, as well as offering numerous breads that brighten *any* festive occasion. In addition, I've included tips on holiday breadbaking that will make a baker's work easier and yield tastier results.

One goal I hope to accomplish here is to turn breads from being an afterthought (as they often are on festive occasions) into a highlight. Many of the breads described on these pages make handsome centerpieces for the holiday meal or snacks that both look and taste great. You'll be delighted at the effect.

And, of course, there is nothing that says a festive bread has to be served only on a certain day or at a certain season! Many people will prefer these breads to cakes or heavy desserts. So offer these festive breads whenever you're in a mood to see the faces of family and friends light up at a display of gourmet breadbaking!

(Do you have a holiday bread recipe not in this book? Please send a copy to me c/o Barron's (address on copyright page). I'll acknowledge all responses and use only with credit to you.)

Important—Every recipe in this book can easily be doubled without changing the baking times. Why not make two loaves and put one in the freezer to enjoy later?

Acknowledgments—My special thanks go to Carole Berglie, project editor, for her expert help in the production of this book; and to Pam Rabin for a splendid job of copyediting the manuscript.

The Festive Bread Book

Chapter 1

Tips on Making Bread

*B*readbaking is an art, and holiday breads are the summit of this art. For centuries, master bakers have shown their greatest skill in preparing breads for feast days and other special occasions. The magnificent breads they developed, appearing in this book, are a tribute to their genius.

Yet you don't have to be an expert to make good bread. This chapter offers tips that will enable any baker to create bread that is a pleasure to make and a joy to eat.

*W*hat are the basic ingredients in breads?

All-purpose flour—contains gluten, a protein that stretches to hold the gas bubbles formed by yeast fermentation. As James Beard says, gluten "creates the architectural plan of the bread."

In general, I recommend unbleached all-purpose flour. This is high in protein and provides good gluten strength. All recipes in this book use all-purpose (white) flour, unless otherwise noted.

Bread flour—slightly more expensive but higher in gluten content, used by most professional bread bakers. Potassium bromate (a chemical usually added to it as a dough conditioner) is intended to make this dough easier to handle. Some people feel that bread made with the flour has better flavor. But I don't find that much difference in kneading or in flavor.

If you wish, give bread flour a try. You may be one of those who feels it is worth the extra cost. Just keep in mind that you will need more water than with all-purpose flour. (If you use bread flour in the recipes of this book, you may require slightly less flour than called for.)

Whole wheat flour is high in protein, but rarely used in holiday breads, which are characteristically fancy and white. (Rye, not a wheat flour, comes mixed with all-purpose flour to add gluten content. Several recipes in this book call for such rye flour.)

NOTE: Don't use *self-rising flour* in yeast breads since it has leavening agents and other additives that interfere with breadbaking. *Bleached flour*, chemically treated to look white, is not recommended.

Store white flour in airtight container in a dry place. Flours other than white should be stored in airtight containers in the refrigerator for relatively short periods, or in the freezer for longer periods.

Measure the larger amount of white flour the recipe calls for into a bowl. Occasionally you will have to use more; but usually you won't use it all. Too much flour will cause your bread to be dry. Bread recipes have approximate amounts of flour because flour absorbs various amounts of liquid. For example, more flour is required on humid days than on dry days.

Yeast—used to make the dough rise. This is a plant microorganism that responds to feeding and warmth. It feeds on starches or sugar, and only lives between the temperatures of 32°F and 130°F. In dough, yeast gives off gas that leavens the bread, or makes it rise.

There are two forms of yeast: active dry yeast and compressed, or cake, yeast. Compressed yeast comes in 0.6-ounce cakes—the equivalent of one tablespoon (one package) of active dry yeast. I prefer the active dry form because it keeps longer than the compressed.

Compressed yeast should be crumbled before using. To soften yeast for use, dissolve it in lukewarm water (80°–90°F) for compressed yeast, and warm water (105°–115°F) for active dry yeast. Put 1 teaspoon of sugar in the water if you want the yeast to dissolve faster.

When adding active dry yeast to flour, the water should be hot (120°–130°F). A candy thermometer can be used to test temperature. With some experience you'll learn to judge the correct temperature by touch.

Yeast may not bubble if the water is too cold or too hot; or the yeast may be too old. *Do not use yeast if it doesn't bubble.*

Sweetening—white, brown, or raw sugar; molasses or honey, depending on the recipe. This activates the yeast while enhancing the flavor.

Liquids—usually water, to dissolve the yeast. But milk provides a smoother, richer flavor. Warm before using (see *Yeast* above).

Fats—butter, margarine, lard, oil, or vegetable shortening. These add flavor and tenderness.

Salt—controls the growth of yeast and helps bring out the flavor of bread.

Eggs—large eggs are used in the recipes throughout this book. These add flavor and texture; make bread more nourishing.

Is it necessary to knead bread?

Some breadmakers have claimed that kneading is not necessary. But I've found that you can't have excellent bread without kneading. This step develops a gluten network throughout the dough and blends the ingredients. Furthermore, kneading is a good way to work off your tensions.

How to Knead

Always knead on a lightly floured surface. Sprinkle flour on surface and hands. Place dough on the surface and fold toward you. Using heels of the hands, push dough down and away. Give dough a quarter turn. Repeat these steps, beginning with folding. Continue until dough is smooth and elastic. Usually the process takes 5 to 10 minutes. But heavy, rich dough may require 15 minutes. Don't worry about overkneading. The dough should have a slightly moist feeling.

Press finger into dough; if dent pops out, dough is kneaded enough. Finished dough is not sticky or dry, but springy.

Rising

Form dough into a ball and place in a lightly greased bowl. When letting the dough rise, be sure to turn over to coat the top. This prevents a crust from forming. Cover with a dish towel. Then place in a warm, draft-free spot. For example: the upper shelf of an oven, with a pan of hot water on the shelf below. Or fill a large pan with hot water and place the bowl of dough on a rack set on top of the pan. Or place a towel over a warm heating pad and put the bowl of dough on top of that. Other places may be used, but be sure they're not too hot or you'll cook the dough.

Let dough rise until it doubles in volume. To check if it has risen enough, put two fingers half an inch into the dough. If a dent remains, dough is properly doubled.

Sometimes I've been right in the middle of baking when my son or daughter came running into the house with a skinned knee. Here are some tricks I use to cope with such interruptions. You'll find that they work for you too.

• A few hours before shaping dough—place the dough in a greased bowl, turning to coat top. Cover and place in the refrigerator 2 to 24 hours. You will have to punch down dough after about 8 hours.

• For a few hours after shaping dough—cover and put in refrigerator. Place on counter for 10 minutes while preheating oven.

Punch down dough in center with your fist. This makes texture firmer by releasing large bubbles. Then knead again for a minute or two to release more bubbles. (If you wish an especially fine texture, let dough rise in bowl a second time.) Now you're ready to shape.

• A few minutes after making dough—shape into a ball; place an inverted bowl over top.

R esting

If recipe calls for this step, put dough on a lightly floured board. Knead for a couple of minutes. Shape into ball, and cover with inverted mixing bowl for about 10 minutes. This process relaxes the gluten and makes dough easier to handle.

S haping

For a *rectangular* loaf, roll dough out gently in one direction with a rolling pin. Make its length less than the length of the bread pan. Roll dough up very tight—otherwise holes in it may cause bubbles during baking. Pinch dough down center to form a lengthwise seam and then pinch end to form end seams. Place in greased pan with the seam side down. Push gently to smooth dough and cause it to touch all four sides of the pan.

If the loaf is too long to put in the loaf pan, cut enough off to make it fit. Bake the extra piece on a greased baking sheet.

For a *round* loaf, shape dough into a ball, place on a baking sheet, and flatten a little bit. If desired, make two or three parallel cuts across top of dough or cut an X.

For *twisting*, make two ropes of equal size. Twist loosely together. Pinch ends together and tuck under.

For *three-rope braiding*, roll out three equal ropes of dough 1 to 2 inches thick to desired length. Start with ropes crossed in middle. Cross right rope over center rope. Cross left rope over new center rope. Then continue (like braiding hair). Turn loaf halfway around and resume braiding. Pinch ends of braids together and tuck under.

You can do some more elaborate braiding if you wish—with four, five, or six ropes of dough. In the following directions, 1 is always the left-most rope; 2, 3, and the others always follow in order. *Thus the number of any one rope changes as you braid with it.* (For example: if rope 1 crosses over rope 4, then rope 1 becomes 4 and rope 4 becomes 3 and so on.) Here are the directions to follow.

Four-Rope Braid

1 over 4 (to right)

3 over 1 (to left)

4 over 3 (between 2 and 3)

2 over 4 (to right)

1 over 2 (between 2 and 3)

Repeat 3 over 1 and down the list, resuming with 3 over 1 until there are no ropes left. Then pinch ends of braids together and tuck under.

Five-Rope Braid

2 over 3 (between 3 and 4)

5 over 2 (between 1 and 2)

1 over 3 (between 3 and 4)

Repeat the list until there are no ropes left. Then pinch ends of braids together and tuck under.

Six-Rope Braid

2 over 6 (far right)

1 over 3 (between 3 and 4)

5 over 1 (far left)

6 over 4 (between 3 and 4)

Repeat the list until there are no ropes left. Then pinch ends of braids together and tuck under.

For *Jacob's Ladder*, roll out two equal ropes of dough. Lay one rope crosswise over the center of the other one. Take opposite ends of bottom one and cross the ends over center so ends change places. Then do the same with other two ropes. And continue, alternating. (Braiding builds vertically rather than horizontally.) Pinch ends and tuck under. (See drawing.)

If you want your ladder twice as long, have four ropes (same size as above) meet in a cross with center ends overlapping slightly. Follow procedure given above. (If you wish, you can bake your Jacob's Ladder in a baking pan rather than on a baking sheet.)

Allow shaped loaf to rise until it doubles in size or until it holds dent made when a finger is gently pressed against its side. A third sign that it has risen enough can be the rising of the center of the dough an inch above the top of the pan.

*B*aking

Here are some rules of thumb that will help your baking go more smoothly.

• Most baking pans are metal; but if you use a glass pan, lower temperature of oven 25°F.

- To determine whether bread is done, tap the top and bottom of the loaf. A hollow sound means it's done.

- When a bread browns too fast, place foil loosely over top.

- If the crust is too hard, brush warm loaf with melted butter.

- If, when you cut the bread, it's not completely done, return to oven for about 5 minutes.

- Cool bread on a wire rack so it does not become soggy in its own steam.

- Make sure you allow bread to cool before cutting. Otherwise texture won't be firm enough.

- It's best to slice breads with fruits in them the day after baking.

Common Mistakes and What to Do About Them

Say your loaf isn't perfect. Maybe the crust is cracked or the texture not quite right. You can learn from the experience and avoid such flaws in the future. Just follow these tips.

- Wrong-size pan: You may use a pan smaller than specified, but don't fill the pan more than two-thirds full. Or if your pan is too small, you may bake the leftover dough on a greased baking sheet.

- When a free-form loaf spreads too much on the baking sheet, usually you haven't used enough flour. Add more flour another time.

- If the bread has a crack or cracks on the top, you may be making one of three mistakes. You may be putting in too much flour, not mixing the dough enough, or not letting the dough rise long enough.

- If the loaf has large holes in it, the dough may not have been mixed enough. Or the dough may have risen more than it should.

- If the crust turns out too dark, the oven was too hot or you used too much sugar or glaze. (Foil over the top of the loaf will help prevent the crust from turning out dark.)

- If the top of the loaf is too pale, your oven temperature may have been too low. Or you may not have used enough sugar. Try placing the pan in the middle of the oven so heat circulates around it.

- If the bottom and sides of the loaf are too pale, you still may improve this loaf. Remove from pan and place directly on oven rack. Bake for another 5 minutes. Test for doneness. If still not done, return to oven for another 5 minutes.

Sourdough

Now for a word about sourdough, which you will find useful in many kinds of breadbaking. Sourdough is sour fermented dough used as leaven. Don't be put off by the name—sourdough breads don't taste sour (though a few people say so). They have a tangy flavor.

Sourdough is a white substance over which a colorless or gray liquor, called *hooch*, collects. Hooch enables sourdough to complete its fermentation. You have to feed sourdough and keep it in the refrigerator because it is a living thing—full of microorganisms. Colonies of these microorganisms can live for many decades with proper care and feeding, and some bakers have vintage batches (mine dates from 1900). You can use a starter batch obtained from someone else to get your own going, buy a dehydrated starter, or make it from scratch. There are many different kinds of sourdough starters—white, yogurt, whole wheat, sour rye, etc. Here's a sourdough starter recipe I recommend to my students.

Sourdough Starter

1 tablespoon active dry yeast

3 cups warm water (105°–115°F)

3½ cups flour

1 Dissolve yeast in warm water in a large mixing bowl. Set aside for about 5 minutes.

2 Gradually add flour, stirring until smooth with a wooden spoon.

3 Cover with cheesecloth; leave on counter in warm, draft-free place. In about 24 hours the mixture will start to ferment.

4 Cover tightly with plastic wrap and leave for another 2 to 3 days. Stir starter 2 or 3 times a day.

5 Starter should be foamy at the end of this time. Put into a plastic container, glass jar, or crock with at least a 1-quart capacity. Stir; cover, but not with tight-fitting top.

Feeding Sourdough

Put 1 cup sourdough in mixing bowl. Add 2½ cups flour and 2 cups warm water. (This is known as feeding.) Mix thoroughly. Leave on counter for 8 hours or overnight. *Be sure to replace 1 cup sourdough in the crock in the refrigerator.* Try to feed sourdough once a week or every 10 days. Feeding is necessary to keep it alive and may add tang to flavor. (Note that sourdough can be frozen.)

General Rules Pertaining to Sourdough

1 Use glass, stoneware, or plastic bowls. (Don't use metal. Wild yeast produces acids that can corrode metal and thus kill the starter.)

2 Use a wooden spoon.

3 Clean container about every week so that unwanted bacteria will not grow and ruin your sourdough.

4 Wipe up spilled sourdough immediately. It can stick like glue or cement.

5 Keep covered with a loose-fitting cover in refrigerator.

Conversion facts

The recipes in this book are designed principally for use in the United States, but can be successfully followed with the ingredients available in other countries. To convert a recipe, consider the following:

Flour—U.S. all-purpose flour, which is used most often in these recipes—is a blending of soft and hard wheat flours. To substitute 100 percent hard wheat flour, be prepared to add a little more water or milk, since high-protein flour absorbs more liquid. You will have to slowly add a small amount of extra liquid (the type of liquid depends on what is specified in the recipe) until the dough is the desired consistency.

Yeast—The U.S. active dry yeast is dual-purpose, in that it can be added directly to the flour mixture or can be dissolved first. In some countries, such as Canada, there are two types of yeast: *fast-rising yeast* and *fast-mixing yeast*. The former is more common, but does not give good results when added directly to the flour. The latter is a type of yeast that is less common, which can be substituted for the U.S. variety. Should you be working with fast-rising yeast, we recommend that you first sprinkle the yeast over warm water in which 1 to 3 teaspoons of sugar have been dissolved, and leave the mixture to sit for 10 minutes. Then continue with the recipe.

Conversion Tables

The following are conversion tables and other information for converting these recipes for use in other English-speaking countries. The cup and spoon measures given in this book are U.S. Customary; use these tables when working with British Imperial or metric kitchen utensils.

Liquid Measures—The old Imperial pint is larger than the U.S. pint; therefore note the following when measuring liquid ingredients.

U.S.

	Imperial
1 cup = 8 fluid ounces	1 cup = 10 fluid ounces
½ cup = 4 fluid ounces	½ cup = 5 fluid ounces
1 tablespoon = ¾ fluid ounce	1 tablespoon = 1 fluid ounce

U.S. Measure	Metric	Imperial*
1 quart	946 ml	1½+ pints
1 pint	473 ml	¾+ pint
1 cup	236 ml	–½ pint
1 tablespoon	15 ml	–1 tablespoon
1 teaspoon	5 ml	–1 teaspoon

*Note that exact quantities cannot always be given. Differences are more crucial when dealing with larger quantities. For teaspoon and tablespoon measures, simply use scant quantities, or for more accurate conversions rely on metric measures.

Weight and Volume Measures—U.S. cooking procedures usually measure certain items by volume, although in the Metric or Imperial systems they are measured by weight. Here are some approximate equivalents for basic items appearing in this book.

	U.S. Customary	Metric	Imperial
Butter	1 cup	250 g	8 ounces
	½ cup	125 g	4 ounces
	¼ cup	62 g	2 ounces
	1 tablespoon	15 g	½ ounce
Flour (sifted all-purpose)	1 cup	128 g	4¼ ounces
	½ cup	60 g	2⅛ ounces
	¼ cup	32 g	1 ounce
Nut meats	1 cup	112 g	4 ounces
Raisins (or Sultanas)	¾ cup	125 g	4 ounces
Sugar: Granulated (Caster)	1 cup	240 g	8 ounces
	½ cup	120 g	4 ounces
	¼ cup	60 g	2 ounces
	1 tablespoon	15 g	½ ounce
Confectioners' (Icing)	1 cup	140 g	5 ounces
	½ cup	70 g	3 ounces
	¼ cup	35 g	1+ ounces
	1 tablespoon	10 g	¼ ounce
Brown	1 cup	160 g	5⅓ ounces
	½ cup	80 g	2⅔ ounces
	¼ cup	40 g	1⅓ ounces
	1 tablespoon	10 g	⅓ ounce

*So as to avoid awkward measurements, some conversions are not exact.

Chapter 2

The New Year

January 1

*T*he Scots call New Year's Eve "Hogmanay." In some parts of Scotland, children traditionally go from door to door, singing this plea for holiday bread:

> *Hogmanay, Trollolay,*
> *Hogmanay, Trollolay,*
> *Give us of your white bread,*
> *And none of your gray!*

*T*he eating of a special bread goes with the New Year's celebration in many countries. In parts of England, a loaf of bread was traditionally broken against a door on New Year's. People rushed to eat the fragments in hopes of warding off hunger during the coming year.

*G*reeks call their New Year's Day "St. Basil's Day" after the great father of the early Church and serve a bread in the saint's honor. As the clock finishes striking midnight New Year's Eve, families divide their St. Basil's bread—vasilopita. The first piece is reserved for the saint, the second piece is set aside for the poor, and the third piece goes to the eldest person in the family. All wait eagerly to see who gets the piece with a lucky gold or silver coin in it.

*I*n this chapter you will find two superb recipes for vasilopita. Other recipes here come from Holland, England, Switzerland, and the United States itself. Offer one with your New Year's meal, or serve it as a snack at a New Year's party or open-house. Your guests will love you for it!

Hogmanay (hog-muh-NAY) Bread

Hogmanay bread, or "black bun," is part of the traditional New Year's celebration in Scotland. Try this fruit and nut bread once, and you'll know why it's recalled so fondly by the Scots. Yields 1 loaf.

Ingredients

¼ cup	chopped candied orange peel
¼ cup	chopped candied lemon peel
3 tablespoons	chopped almonds
3 tablespoons	dark raisins soaked in hot water for 10 minutes and drained
3 tablespoons	currants soaked in hot water for 10 minutes and drained
¼ teaspoon	grated nutmeg
½ teaspoon	ground ginger
¼ teaspoon	ground cloves
2 tablespoons	rum or brandy
2½–3 cups	flour
½ tablespoon	active dry yeast
½ teaspoon	salt
4 tablespoons	unsalted butter, softened
⅔ cup	hot water (120°–130°F)

Preparation

1 Soak orange peel, lemon peel, almonds, raisins, currants, and spices in rum or brandy for 2 hours. (You may prefer soaking the fruit overnight.)

2 Combine 2 cups flour, yeast, salt, butter, and hot water. Mix well.

3 Add enough remaining flour to form a soft dough. Knead on lightly floured surface until smooth—about 10 minutes. Place in greased bowl, turning to coat top.

4 Cover; let rise in warm place until double—about 1 hour.

5 Punch down dough. Reserve ⅓ dough. Cover and set aside.

6 Knead in the fruit. Make a 6-inch ball.

7 Using the ⅓ dough reserved, make a 12-inch circle. Place fruit ball in center of this circle and fold dough over it.

8 Grease an 8-inch cake pan. Flatten and pierce dough completely through all over with skewer or something similar. (This allows the steam to escape during baking.) Place in pan.

9 Bake in a preheated 350°F oven 1½ hours. It is necessary to remove from pan the last 20 minutes and continue baking to brown the sides. Cool on wire rack.

• **Note:** This bread has a lot of fruit. You may prefer reducing the amount of fruit by one-third.

Vasilopita (vas-e-LOH-pee-tah) I—St. Basil's Bread

St. Basil's bread is enjoyable apart from the beautiful Greek ceremony that accompanies it. Your guests can have fun seeing who gets the lucky almond (my suggested substitute for the traditional coin). The first recipe is the spicier; the second, with a delicious taste of its own, is more decorative. Each recipe yields 1 loaf.

Ingredients

1 tablespoon	active dry yeast
¼ cup	warm water (105°–115°F)
½ cup	warm milk (105°–115°F)
½ cup	sugar
½ teaspoon	salt
4 tablespoons	unsalted butter, melted
2	eggs, beaten
½ tablespoon	grated lemon peel
¼ teaspoon	ground cinnamon
½ teaspoon	grated nutmeg
⅛ teaspoon	ground cloves
2½–3 cups	flour
1	whole almond, if desired
	unsalted butter, softened
	sesame seeds

Glaze

1	egg, beaten with 1 tablespoon water

Preparation

1 Dissolve yeast in warm water. Set aside for 5 minutes.

2 Combine warm milk, sugar, salt, butter, eggs, lemon peel, and spices in a large mixing bowl.

3 Add 1½ cups flour and yeast mixture. Beat until smooth. Add enough remaining flour to make a soft dough.

4 Knead on lightly floured surface until smooth—about 10 minutes.

5 Place the dough in lightly greased bowl, turning to coat top. Cover and let rise in warm place until double—about 1½ hours.

6 Punch down dough. You can knead a whole almond into the dough at this point if you wish. (A coin might crack a tooth!) Set aside 10 minutes to rest.

7 Brush 1½-quart soufflé dish or 10-inch cake pan with soft butter. Sprinkle sesame seeds in dish or pan.

8 Make dough into a ball and place in bowl; press down so dough covers the bottom.

9 Cover; let rise in warm place until double—about 1 hour. Make glaze and brush on loaf. Sprinkle top with sesame seeds.

10 Bake in a preheated 350°F oven for about 45 minutes or until done. Cool on wire rack.

Vasilopita II

Ingredients

2–2½ cups	flour
½ tablespoon	active dry yeast
¾ teaspoon	lemon peel
½ teaspoon	aniseeds
½ cup	milk
4 tablespoons	unsalted butter
2 tablespoons	sugar
½ teaspoon	salt
1	egg
	sesame seeds

Glaze

1	egg yolk, beaten with 1 tablespoon water

Preparation

1 Combine 1 cup flour, yeast, lemon peel, and aniseeds. Heat milk, butter, sugar, and salt to hot (120°–130°F).

2 Add milk mixture to dry ingredients; add egg. Mix thoroughly.

3 Stir in enough remaining flour to form a soft dough. Knead on lightly floured surface until smooth—about 10 minutes.

4 Place in greased bowl, turning to coat top. Cover; let rise in warm place until double—about 1½ hours.

5 Punch down dough. Flatten half of the dough in greased 8-inch round cake pan. Shape other half into 2 ropes each 18 inches long. Fold ropes in half and twist. Join ends and seal to make 7-inch circle. Then place on top of flat circle of dough.

6 Make glaze and brush on loaf. Sprinkle with sesame seeds.

7 Let rise in warm place until double—about 30 minutes.

8 Bake in a preheated 375°F oven 30–40 minutes or until done. Cool on wire rack.

Oliebollen, pages 21 and 22 ▶

Oliebollen (OH-lee-bow-len) I

Dutch by origin, these doughnuts became an American favorite in eighteenth-century New York. You'll find them a delight for New Year's Eve snacking. The following two recipes are similar, but the first includes candied fruit and the second includes fresh apple and cream. This recipe yields 20 doughnuts.

Ingredients

¼ cup	milk
3 tablespoons	sugar
3 tablespoons	unsalted butter
¼ teaspoon	salt
1–1½ cups	flour
½ tablespoon	active dry yeast
1	egg
1	egg yolk
3 tablespoons	dark raisins
3 tablespoons	chopped mixed candied fruit
	vegetable oil for deep frying
3 tablespoons	sugar
½ teaspoon	ground cinnamon

Preparation

1 Heat milk, sugar, butter, and salt to hot (120°–130°F). Combine ¾ cup flour and yeast in mixing bowl.

2 Combine flour mixture, milk mixture, egg, and egg yolk. Mix thoroughly.

3 Add enough remaining flour to form a soft dough. Knead on lightly floured surface until smooth—about 10 minutes.

4 Place in greased bowl, turning to coat top. Cover; let rise in warm place until double—about 30 minutes.

5 Knead in raisins and candied fruit. Let rest for 10 minutes. Shape into 20 equal balls. Heat vegetable oil to 375°F. Using a slotted spoon, carefully drop the balls (5 or 6 at a time) into the oil. Fry about 3 minutes, turning until golden brown all over.

6 Drain on several paper towels. Combine sugar and cinnamon, and dust doughnuts while warm. (I often dust doughnuts by shaking them in a lunch-size paper bag with this mixture.)

Oliebollen II

This recipe yields 24 doughnuts.

Ingredients

2½–3 cups	flour
½ tablespoon	active dry yeast
3 tablespoons	sugar
¼ teaspoon	salt
½ teaspoon	grated lemon peel
¼ cup	milk
⅔ cup	light cream
2 tablespoons	unsalted butter
2	egg yolks
1 cup	coarsely grated apples
⅓ cup	golden raisins
¼ cup	chopped candied lemon peel
	vegetable oil for deep frying

Preparation

1 Combine 2 cups flour, yeast, sugar, salt, and lemon peel in mixing bowl. Heat milk, cream, and butter to hot (120°–130°F).

2 Combine flour mixture, cream mixture, and egg yolks. Mix thoroughly. Add apples, raisins, and candied lemon peel.

3 Add enough remaining flour to make a soft dough. Knead on lightly floured surface until smooth—about 10 minutes.

4 Place in greased bowl, turning to coat top. Cover; let rise in warm place until double—about 45–60 minutes. Heat vegetable oil to 375°F.

5 Knead dough for about 3 minutes. Form dough into balls about the size of a walnut. Fry until crisp and brown on all sides.

6 Remove with slotted spoon and drain on paper towels. While still warm, coat with confectioners' sugar. (You can dust doughnuts by shaking them with confectioners' sugar in a lunch-size paper bag.)

English Pope Ladies

Much of the charm of these buns comes from their ladylike shape. They are said to be named after the mythical Pope Joan (around 858 A.D.). Pope Ladies are a traditional New Year's treat in England. Yields 12 buns.

Ingredients

1 tablespoon	active dry yeast
2 tablespoons	warm water (105°–115°F)
¼ cup	milk
1 stick	unsalted butter
3 tablespoons	sugar
¼ teaspoon	salt
3–3½ cups	flour
1	egg
	currants or dark raisins

Glaze

1	egg, beaten with 1 tablespoon water

Preparation

1 Dissolve yeast in warm water. Set aside for 5 minutes. Heat milk, butter, sugar, and salt to warm (105°–115°F).

2 Combine 2 cups flour, yeast mixture, milk mixture, and 1 egg in bowl. Mix thoroughly.

3 Add enough remaining flour to make a soft dough. Knead on lightly floured surface until smooth—about 10 minutes.

4 Place in greased bowl, turning to coat top. Cover; let rise in warm place until double—about 1 hour.

5 Punch down dough. Divide into 12 equal balls about 2½ inches across. Cut each ball in half. Flatten one of the halves and shape into an oval for the body. Divide the other half of dough in two; make a round ball for head. With remaining dough make pencil-like ropes 4 inches long. Cut in half for 2 arms. Press head and arms to body. (There are no legs.) Press raisins or currants deeply in place for the eyes and nose. See drawing.

6 Let rise in warm place until double—about 30 minutes. Make glaze and brush on buns.

7 Bake in a preheated 350°F oven about 15–20 minutes or until done. Cool on wire rack.

Swiss Braid

For a lighter New Year's bread, you should try this lemon-flavored braid from Switzerland. A three-rope braid is suggested in the recipe, but you can also use one of the more elaborate braids described in Chapter 1. Yields 1 loaf.

Ingredients

½ tablespoon	active dry yeast
2 tablespoons	warm water (105°–115°F)
¼ cup	milk
3 tablespoons	unsalted butter
3 tablespoons	sugar
¼ teaspoon	salt
1½–2 cups	flour
1 tablespoon	lemon juice
½ teaspoon	grated lemon peel
1	egg
¼ cup	golden raisins
Glaze	
1	egg, beaten with 1 tablespoon water

Preparation

1 Dissolve yeast in warm water. Set aside for 5 minutes. Heat milk, butter, sugar, and salt to warm (105°–115°F).

2 Combine 1 cup flour, yeast mixture, milk mixture, lemon juice, and lemon peel in mixing bowl. Mix thoroughly.

3 Add egg, raisins, and enough remaining flour to make a soft dough. Knead on lightly floured surface until smooth—about 10 minutes.

4 Place in greased bowl, turning to coat top. Cover; let rise in warm place until double—about 1 hour.

5 Punch down dough. Divide dough into 3 equal pieces. Braid and place on greased baking sheet.

6 Cover; let rise in warm place until double—about 45 minutes.

7 Make glaze and brush on loaf. Bake in a preheated 350°F oven about 45–55 minutes or until done. Cool on wire rack.

New Year's Rolls

You'll enjoy this delicate lemon-flavored bread with coffee or tea for a festive snack. Make rolls ahead and freeze until ready to use for your New Year's gathering. Yields 12 rolls.

Ingredients

½ cup	milk
⅔ cup	sugar
4 tablespoons	unsalted butter, softened
¼ teaspoon	salt
2–2½ cups	flour
½ tablespoon	active dry yeast
1	egg
1 teaspoon	grated lemon peel
½ teaspoon	ground cardamom

Icing

⅔ cup	confectioners' sugar
2 tablespoons	milk

Preparation

1 Heat milk, ⅓ cup sugar, 2 tablespoons butter, and salt to hot (120°–130°F). Combine 1½ cups flour and yeast.

2 Add egg and enough remaining flour to make a soft dough. Knead on lightly floured surface until smooth—about 10 minutes.

3 Place in greased bowl, turning to coat top. Cover; let rise in warm place until double—about 1 hour.

4 Punch down dough. Cover with inverted bowl; let rest for 10 minutes.

5 Roll into 8 x 12-inch rectangle. Cream ⅓ cup sugar and 2 tablespoons butter with lemon peel and cardamom. Spread over dough.

6 Roll up jelly-roll style. Slice crosswise into 12 pieces. Place cut side down in greased muffin pans.

7 Cover; let rise in warm place until double—about 30 minutes.

8 Bake in a preheated 375°F oven about 20 minutes or until done.

9 Make icing by mixing confectioners' sugar and milk until smooth. Drizzle over warm rolls. Cool on wire rack.

Rum Rolls

You and your guests will love the hint of rum in these rolls. Make ahead of time, if you wish, and freeze until New Year's. Yields 12 rolls.

Ingredients

½ cup	sugar
½ teaspoon	salt
3 tablespoons	unsalted butter
½ cup	milk
1 tablespoon	active dry yeast
¼ cup	warm water (105°–115°F)
2½–3 cups	flour
1	egg
1½ tablespoons	light rum
	unsalted butter, melted
½ teaspoon	grated nutmeg
	chopped pecans

Icing

¾ cup	confectioners' sugar
2 tablespoons	light rum

Preparation

1 Heat ¼ cup sugar, salt, butter, and milk to warm (105°–115°F).

2 Dissolve yeast in warm water. Set aside for 5 minutes. Add 2 cups flour, yeast mixture, egg, and rum to milk mixture. Mix thoroughly.

3 Add enough remaining flour to form a soft dough. Knead on lightly floured surface until smooth—about 10 minutes. Place in greased bowl, turning to coat top.

4 Cover; let rise in warm place until double—about 1 hour.

5 Punch down dough. Roll into a rectangle about 8 x 16 inches. Brush with melted butter.

6 Combine ¼ cup sugar with nutmeg. Sprinkle on dough. Working from the wide side, roll up tight in jelly-roll style. Cut roll into pieces 1½ inches wide.

7 Place cut side up in buttered muffin pans. Brush tops with melted butter. Cover; let rise until double—about 30 minutes.

8 Bake in a preheated 375°F oven 25 to 30 minutes or until done. To make frosting, mix confectioners' sugar and light rum until smooth.

9 Remove from muffin pan. While warm, frost with the icing. Sprinkle with chopped nuts.

Chapter 3

Twelfth Night (Epiphany)

January 6

Since Twelfth Night concludes the Christmas holidays, people traditionally have marked it with a big party closing the season. The Twelfth Night revels in many countries feature parties, dancing, and feasting. At the feasts, people often eat a special bread or cake with a bean, coin, or figurine baked in it. The person getting the piece with the good luck token becomes the Twelfth Night King or Queen, leading revelers in their merrymaking.

The holiday also carries solemn religious overtones. It is one of the three major Christian holidays, along with Christmas and Easter. The name Twelfth Night simply reflects its occurrence twelve days after Christmas. But in some places it is known as Feast of the Three Kings because the Three Kings (also known as Wise Men or Magi) are believed to have reached the Christ Child on January 6. And, with emphasis on the religious character of the occasion, Epiphany notes that the holiday marks a special revelation of Jesus's divine nature—the arrival of the three Magi as the first manifestation of Jesus to the Gentiles.

The breads baked for Twelfth Night are delicious and varied. In this chapter you'll find recipes harking to Merrie Olde England, Mexico and Spain, Brazil, France, and Holland. Note the lucky tokens in several of the breads. They never fail to add to the merriment of Twelfth Night parties! (Be sure to warn your guests not to bite down too hard until any token is found.)

You may not choose to stage a full Twelfth Night celebration, but the breads in this chapter will add a distinctive and richly historical touch to the end of your Christmas holidays.

Twelfth Night Bread I

Here's a traditional bread for your own Twelfth Night revels. The first recipe is baked in a Bundt pan; the second has a ring shape. Add to the fun of this bread by including two porcelain figurines (ideally a king and a queen). Wrap them in tin foil and insert while shaping dough. Yields 1 cake.

Ingredients

½ tablespoon	active dry yeast
3 tablespoons	warm water (105°–115°F)
⅓ cup	evaporated milk
2–2½ cups	flour
6 tablespoons	unsalted butter, softened
¼ cup	sugar
½ teaspoon	salt
1	egg
	Confectioners' Icing (p. 208)
	additional nuts and candied cherries

Filling

½ cup	candied cherries
⅓ cup	chopped Brazil nuts or walnuts
1 teaspoon	grated orange peel

Preparation

1 Dissolve yeast in warm water. Add milk and ½ cup flour. Set aside; let rise until double—about 30 minutes.

2 Combine butter, sugar, salt, egg, and yeast mixture in mixing bowl. Mix thoroughly.

3 Add enough remaining flour to make a soft dough. Knead on lightly floured surface until smooth—about 10 minutes.

4 Place in greased bowl, turning to coat top. Cover; let rise in warm place until double—about 1 hour.

5 Combine cherries, nuts, and orange peel in small bowl. Roll dough into rectangle 6 x 9 inches. Spread fruit mixture evenly over the dough.

6 Shape into a ball, make a hole in the center, and place in greased 6-cup Bundt pan. Cover; let rise almost to top of pan in warm place—about 30 minutes.

7 Bake in a preheated 350°F oven 45 minutes or until done. Cool on wire rack.

8 Drizzle Confectioners' Icing over cooled bread. Decorate with nuts and candied cherries.

Twelfth Night Bread II

Yields 1 ring.

Ingredients

½ tablespoon	active dry yeast
¼ cup	warm water (105°–115°F)
¼ cup	milk
3 tablespoons	sugar
½ teaspoon	salt
3 tablespoons	unsalted butter
1½–2 cups	flour
2	egg yolks
	unsalted butter, melted
	confectioners' sugar

Filling

½ cup	cinnamon sugar
	chopped Brazil nuts or walnuts
½ cup	chopped mixed candied fruit

Preparation

1 Dissolve yeast in warm water. Set aside for 5 minutes. Heat milk, sugar, salt, and butter to warm (105°–115°F).

2 Combine 1½ cups flour, milk mixture, yeast mixture, and egg yolks in mixing bowl. Mix thoroughly.

3 Add enough remaining flour to form a soft dough. Knead on lightly floured surface until smooth—about 10 minutes.

4 Place in greased bowl, turning to coat top. Cover; let rise in warm place until double—about 1 hour.

5 Punch down dough. Roll into rectangle 12 x 14 inches.

6 Spread with melted butter. Sprinkle with cinnamon sugar and with nuts and candied fruit.

7 Roll dough into rope about 1½ inches across. Shape into a ring and seal ends together. Place on greased baking sheet.

8 Brush with melted butter. Cover; let rise again until almost double—about 45–60 minutes.

9 Bake in a preheated 350°F oven 30–45 minutes or until done.

10 Cool on wire rack. Dust with confectioners' sugar.

Rosca de Reyes (ROES-ka day RAY-ays)—Kings' Bread Ring

Brighten your Twelfth Night as Mexicans do, with this bread. They say the person whose piece contains an enclosed coin or little doll must give a party on Candlemas Day—February 2. Yields 1 medium ring.

Ingredients

1 teaspoon	dried orange peel
1 tablespoon	light rum
1 tablespoon	active dry yeast
¼ cup	warm water (105°–115°F)
¼ cup	milk
4 tablespoons	sugar
4 tablespoons	unsalted butter
1 teaspoon	salt
2½–3½ cups	flour
2	eggs
	Confectioners' Icing (p. 208)
	candied cherries or candied orange peel, if desired

Preparation

1 Soak orange peel in rum about 30 minutes. Dissolve yeast in warm water.

2 Heat milk, sugar, butter, and salt to warm (105°–115°F).

3 Add 1½ cups flour, eggs, yeast mixture, and the rum-soaked orange peel. Mix thoroughly.

4 Add enough remaining flour to make a soft dough. Knead on lightly floured surface until smooth—about 10 minutes.

5 Here you insert coin or doll if desired. (Just warn your guests!) Roll dough into long rope. Shape into a ring and seal ends together. Place on greased baking sheet.

6 Cover; let rise in warm place until double—about 1 hour.

7 Bake in a preheated 350°F oven 35–45 minutes or until done. Cool on wire rack.

8 Frost with icing and, if desired, decorate with candied cherries or orange peel.

Spanish King's Cake

In Spanish-speaking countries, gifts are exchanged on Twelfth Night rather than on Christmas Day. Along with the gifts often comes this festive bread—which makes a party in itself. Yields 1 twisted loaf.

Ingredients

1 tablespoon	active dry yeast
¼ cup	warm water (105°–115°F)
¼ cup	milk
¼ cup	sugar
4 tablespoons	unsalted butter
½ teaspoon	salt
¼ teaspoon	ground mace
2–2½ cups	flour
1	egg
¼ cup	golden raisins
¼ cup	chopped mixed candied fruit
¼ cup	chopped walnuts
	Confectioners' Icing (p. 208)
	walnut halves
	candied fruit

Preparation

1 Dissolve yeast in warm water. Set aside for 5 minutes. Heat milk, sugar, butter, and salt to warm (105°–115°F).

2 Combine mace, 1½ cups flour, yeast mixture, milk mixture, and egg. Mix thoroughly.

3 Add raisins, mixed candied fruit, and chopped walnuts. Mix thoroughly. Add enough remaining flour to make a soft dough. Knead on lightly floured surface until smooth—about 10 minutes.

4 Place in greased bowl, turning to coat top. Cover; let rise in warm place until double—about 1½ hours.

5 Punch down dough. Divide dough in half. Roll each into a 20-inch rope. Twist together.

6 Place on greased baking sheet. Cover; let rise until almost double—about 45–60 minutes.

7 Bake in a preheated 350°F oven 30 minutes or until done. Cool on wire rack.

8 Frost loaf with Confectioners' Icing and decorate with walnut halves and additional candied fruit.

Brazilian King's Bread

Here's a bread Brazilians love with their coffee on Twelfth Night. The finder of a tiny doll enclosed during shaping becomes king or queen of the holiday celebration. You can substitute a lucky almond for your own party. Yields 1 ring.

Ingredients

½ tablespoon	active dry yeast
2 tablespoons	warm water (105°–115°F)
⅓ cup	milk
3 tablespoons	sugar
¼ teaspoon	salt
3 tablespoons	unsalted butter
2–2½ cups	flour
1	egg
2 tablespoons	golden raisins
2 tablespoons	chopped mixed candied fruit, plus extra for decoration
1 tablespoon	chopped Brazil nuts or blanched almonds
1	whole almond, plus additional for decoration
1 tablespoon	sugar
Glaze	
1	egg, beaten with 1 tablespoon water

Preparation

1 Dissolve yeast in warm water. Set aside for 5 minutes. Heat milk, sugar, salt, and butter to warm (105°–115°F).

2 Combine 1½ cups flour, yeast mixture, milk mixture, and egg. Mix thoroughly.

3 Add enough remaining flour to form a soft dough. Knead on lightly floured surface about 10 minutes.

4 Place in greased bowl, turning to coat top. Cover; let rise in warm place until double—about 1 hour.

5 Lightly knead in raisins, candied fruit, and nuts. Place in greased bowl, turning to coat top. Cover; let rise in warm place until double—about 45 minutes. (This is for the second time.)

6 Punch down dough and insert whole almond. Shape a round loaf; make a 4-inch hole in center and push dough into a ring about 8 inches across. Place on greased baking sheet. (Butter outside of a 3- or 4-inch custard dish and set it in the hole.)

7 Let bread rise in warm place for 30 minutes. Make glaze and brush on loaf. Press lightly with whole candied fruits and whole nuts. Sprinkle top with sugar.

8 Bake in a preheated 350°F oven 40–45 minutes or until done. Cool on wire rack.

Twelfth Night Bread of Lady Carcas

*This orange-flavored bread honors the thwarting of Charlemagne's
siege of Carcassonne by Lady Carcas more than a thousand years ago.
But the bread also is featured in French celebrations of Twelfth Night.
Try it for an especially elegant treat. Yields 1 loaf.*

Ingredients

1 teaspoon	grated orange peel
3 tablespoons	orange juice
1 tablespoon	active dry yeast
2 tablespoons	warm water (105°–115°F)
2½–3 cups	flour
⅓ cup	sugar
½ teaspoon	salt
4	egg yolks
3 tablespoons	unsalted butter, softened

Glaze

1	egg, beaten with 1 tablespoon milk

Preparation

1. Combine orange peel and orange juice. Set aside. Dissolve yeast in warm water. Set aside for 5 minutes.

2. Combine 2 cups flour, sugar, and salt in mixing bowl. Add yeast mixture, 1 egg yolk at a time, and butter. Mix thoroughly.

3. Add orange juice mixture and enough remaining flour to make a soft dough. Knead on lightly floured surface until smooth—about 10 minutes.

4. Make a ball of dough and cover with inverted mixing bowl for 30 minutes.

5. Make a ball and flatten to about 2-inch thickness with hands. Place on greased baking sheet.

6. Cover; let rise for 35–45 minutes. Make glaze and brush on loaf. Pierce dough completely through about 8–10 times with a skewer or something similar.

7. Bake in a preheated 400°F oven about 25–35 minutes or until done. Cool on wire rack.

33

Dutch King's Bread

Want something a little plainer? Try this fragrant Twelfth Night bread, beloved by the Dutch. Contributing to the party atmosphere it creates is the single lucky almond one person will find. Yields 1 loaf.

Ingredients

½ tablespoon	active dry yeast
1 tablespoon	warm water (105°–115°F)
⅓ cup	milk
2 tablespoons	sugar
¼ teaspoon	salt
2 tablespoons	unsalted butter
1¾–2¼ cups	flour
1	egg
1	whole almond
	Confectioners' Icing (p. 208)
	candied cherries

Preparation

1 Dissolve yeast in warm water. Set aside for 5 minutes. Heat milk, sugar, salt, and butter to warm (105°–115°F).

2 Combine 1½ cups flour, yeast mixture, milk mixture, and egg in mixing bowl. Mix thoroughly.

3 Add enough remaining flour to make a soft dough. Knead on lightly floured surface until smooth—about 10 minutes.

4 Put in greased bowl, turning to coat top. Cover; let rise in warm place until double—about 1 hour.

5 Punch down dough. Knead in 1 whole almond.

6 Make a round loaf. Place on greased baking sheet. Cover; let rise in warm place until double—about 45 minutes.

7 Bake in a preheated 350°F oven about 1 hour or until done. Cool on wire rack.

8 Frost with Confectioners' Icing. Decorate with cherries.

Chapter 4

Lincoln's Birthday

February 12

*Y*oung Abe Lincoln first gained fame with his axe. As a gangling but powerful youngster, he chopped down big trees and shaped them into bench boards, barn beams, and fence rails. He was so strong that he could hold out an axe by the end of its handle with thumb and forefinger. People came from miles around to watch his exploits.

*B*ut Lincoln's nickname of "Rail Splitter" did not become nationally known until he was a presidential candidate in the election of 1860. In this campaign, his prowess with the axe came to symbolize both his humble beginnings and his inner strength.

*T*oday we still remember Lincoln for his axemanship as well as his statesmanship, and his birthday inspires many representations of axes and logs. Try the following coffee cake on your family and friends for your own personal celebration of the Rail Splitter.

Lincoln Log Coffee Cake

*This cream cheese-filled "log" should be covered with chocolate
to represent the texture of bark. Watch children of all ages go for it!
Yields 1 loaf.*

Ingredients

2–3 cups	flour
⅓ cup	sugar
½ teaspoon	salt
1 tablespoon	active dry yeast
¼ cup	milk
¼ cup	water
2 tablespoons	unsalted butter
1	egg
	Chocolate Icing (p. 208)

Filling

4 ounces	cream cheese, softened
3 tablespoons	sugar
1	egg yolk

Preparation

1 Combine 1½ cups flour, sugar, salt, and yeast in a large bowl. Heat milk, water, and butter to hot (120–130°F).

2 Add milk mixture to dry ingredients and mix thoroughly. Add egg and enough remaining flour to make a soft dough. Mix thoroughly.

3 Knead on lightly floured surface for about 10 minutes.

4 Place in greased bowl, turning to coat top. Cover; let rise in warm place until double—about 1 hour.

5 Make filling: Cream the cheese with sugar until light and fluffy. Then blend in egg yolk.

6 Punch down dough. Roll dough into a 9 x 12-inch rectangle.

7 Spread with cheese filling, leaving ½ inch of dough all around edge. Roll up jelly-roll style to form 12-inch roll. Seal edges and place on greased baking sheet.

8 Using scissors, cut slits ⅔ through dough at 1-inch intervals.

9 Cover; let rise in warm place until double—about 45 minutes.

10 Bake in a preheated 350°F oven about 25 minutes or until done. Cool on wire rack. Cover with Chocolate Icing to look like bark.

Chapter 5

St. Valentine's Day

February 14

*T*here were actually several St. Valentines, two of them Christian martyrs in third-century Rome. In 496 Pope Gelasius set February 14 as a feast day in their honor. He clearly did not expect the romantic aura that came to surround the date. One reason for this development may have been the ancient Roman fertility festival of Lupercalia that fell on February 15.

*S*t. Valentine's Day has been celebrated in various ways through the ages. Articles of clothing, knickknacks, and books are among the gifts that have been exchanged at this time. One of the more charming customs used to be that of serving special cakes and breads. The heart-shaped breads in this chapter, reviving the festival side of the holiday, are guaranteed to delight a sweetheart or anyone else.

St. Valentine's Day Cake

Here's a heart-shaped cake that says it all. Vary the suggested cherry filling, if you wish, with one of the others in Chapter 20.
Yields 1 cake.

Ingredients

2–2½ cups	flour
1 tablespoon	active dry yeast
⅔ cup	milk
¼ cup	sugar
½ teaspoon	salt
2 tablespoons	unsalted butter
1	egg
	unsalted butter, melted

Filling

½ cup	light brown sugar, firmly packed
⅓ cup	ground almonds
3 tablespoons	chopped maraschino cherries, well drained
¾ teaspoon	almond extract
½ cup	flaked coconut, if desired

Preparation

1 Combine 1½ cups flour and yeast in large bowl. Mix.

2 Heat milk, sugar, salt, and butter to hot (120°–130°F).

3 Add the milk mixture to dry ingredients and mix until smooth. Add egg and enough remaining flour to make a soft dough.

4 Knead on lightly floured surface until smooth—about 10 minutes. Place in greased bowl, turning to coat top.

5 Cover; let rise in warm place until double—about 1 hour.

6 Punch down dough. Roll dough into a 15 x 22-inch rectangle.

7 Brush with melted butter. Combine brown sugar, ground almonds, cherries, almond extract, and coconut in small bowl. Sprinkle over dough.

8 Roll up jelly-roll style. Pinch seam to seal. Gently pull into a 26-inch roll. Place on greased baking sheet. Firmly seal ends together and shape into heart.

9 Along the outside edge of heart, make cuts ⅔ of the way into dough at 1½-inch intervals. Turn each cut section toward its side.

10 Cover; let rise in warm place until double—about 1 hour.

11 Bake in a preheated 350°F oven 25–30 minutes or until done. Cool on wire rack.

Frosting (optional)

1 cup	confectioners' sugar
2–3 tablespoons	milk
4–6 drops	red food coloring

12 If icing is desired, mix confectioners' sugar and milk until smooth. Add coloring for a pink hue. Frost when cool.

Cupid's Coffee Cake

This nut-filled Valentine coffee cake, especially good with breakfast or brunch, will make the day one your sweetheart will never forget. Yields 1 coffee cake.

Ingredients

2 cups	flour
3 tablespoons	sugar
½ teaspoon	salt
1 tablespoon	active dry yeast
½ cup	milk
3 tablespoons	unsalted butter
1	egg
2 tablespoons	unsalted butter, melted

Filling

½ cup	sugar
¾ cup	chopped walnuts or pecans
1½ teaspoons	ground cinnamon

Preparation

1 Combine 1½ cups flour, sugar, salt, and yeast. Heat milk and butter to hot (120°–130°F).

2 Add egg and milk mixture to flour mixture. Mix thoroughly.

3 Add enough remaining flour to form a soft dough. Knead on lightly floured surface until smooth—about 10 minutes.

4 Place in greased bowl, turning to coat top. Cover; let rise in warm place until double—about 1 hour.

5 Punch down dough. On lightly floured surface roll out dough into 10 x 15-inch rectangle.

6 Combine sugar, nuts, and cinnamon. Brush dough with melted butter. Sprinkle with cinnamon mixture. Starting with wide side, roll up jelly-roll style. Pinch seams and ends.

7 Place on greased baking sheet seam side up. Fold half the roll over top of other half, sealing ends together. Cut with scissors from folded end down center of roll to within 1 inch of other end. Make a heart by turning the cut halves out with cut side up.

8 Cover; set in warm place until double—about 1 hour.

9 Bake in a preheated 350°F oven 20–25 minutes or until done. Cool on wire rack.

Chapter 6

Washington's Birthday

February 22

From the earliest years of the Republic, George Washington's birthday has been celebrated widely and often lavishly throughout the United States. Even rural taverns sometimes witnessed parties at which more than a thousand guests danced, ate huge cakes, and toasted the Father of Our Country. In 1795, when the President lived in Philadelphia while the White House was abuilding, Washington presided at his own party. "After walking socially among the company and inquiring about the health of the individuals," a participant wrote, "he opened a door leading into another apartment and, smiling, asked us if we were disposed for a little cake and wine by way of refreshment. The cake was round and nearly three feet in diameter and one in thickness. His wine was excellent and punch high flavored. We all joined in the conviviality, the President mingling and partaking with the company."

An outburst of celebrations on Washington's 250th birthday in 1982 proves that the occasion has lost little of its early luster. Exhibitions, historical tours, concerts, cherry pie eating contests, and parties took place in his honor—over 100 such events in the New York City area alone. To cite one example, children at a party in the Morris-Jumel Mansion in New York City—once the General's military headquarters—made their own colonial costumes, sang "Happy Birthday to George," and blew out the 250 candles on a cherry-topped cake a yard wide.

If a Washington's Birthday party is not accessible to you, stage your own. You can start with one of the contemporary holiday breads in this chapter—two honoring the General and one that paragon of First Ladies, Washington's beloved Martha.

Washington's Coffee Cake

The cherry tree will always be associated in the minds of Americans with George Washington's integrity—though the story behind it is, of course, mere legend. Anyway, here is a cherry-dotted coffee cake that charmingly commemorates the Father of Our Country. Yields 1 loaf.

Ingredients

½ tablespoon	active dry yeast
2 tablespoons	warm water (105°–115°F)
¼ cup	milk
1 tablespoon	sugar
¼ teaspoon	salt
4 tablespoons	unsalted butter
1 cup	flour
1	egg

Filling

⅓ cup	light brown sugar, firmly packed
⅔ cup	pitted tart cherries, fresh, canned, or frozen
¼ cup	chopped pecans
½ teaspoon	vanilla extract
¼ teaspoon	ground cinnamon
¼ teaspoon	ground allspice

Icing

½ cup	confectioners' sugar
1 tablespoon	milk
½ teaspoon	vanilla extract

Preparation

1 Dissolve yeast in warm water. Set aside for 5 minutes. Heat milk, sugar, salt, and 3 tablespoons butter to warm (105°–115°F).

2 Combine yeast mixture, flour, milk mixture, and egg. Knead on lightly floured surface until smooth—about 10 minutes.

3 Place in greased bowl, turning to coat top. Cover; let rise in warm place until double—about 1 hour.

4 Punch down dough. Roll into a 6-inch square. Place on greased baking sheet. Mix filling ingredients.

5 Spread cherry filling down center third. Using scissors, snip sides toward center at 1-inch intervals. Fold strips of dough over filling, alternating from side to side. (See diagram.)

6 Cover; let rise in warm place until double—about 30 minutes.

7 Bake in a preheated 350°F oven about 30–35 minutes. Cool on wire rack. Make icing. Drizzle over coffee cake.

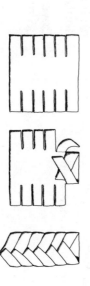

George Washington's Hatchet

My children love this hatchet-shaped, nut-filled coffee cake every time. Yours will enjoy the fun of the cake too. Yields 1 cake.

Ingredients

½ tablespoon	active dry yeast
¼ cup	warm water (105°–115°F)
¼ cup	milk
4 tablespoons	unsalted butter
½ teaspoon	salt
2 tablespoons	sugar
2–2½ cups	flour
1	egg
	candied cherries or maraschino cherries, well drained (optional)

Filling

½ cup	light brown sugar, firmly packed
⅔ cup	chopped walnuts
½ teaspoon	ground cinnamon
4 tablespoons	unsalted butter, melted

Preparation

1 Dissolve yeast in warm water. Set aside for 5 minutes. Heat milk, butter, salt, and sugar to warm (105°–115°F).

2 Combine 1½ cups flour, yeast mixture, milk mixture, and egg. Mix thoroughly.

3 Add enough remaining flour to make a soft dough. Knead on lightly floured surface until smooth—about 10 minutes.

4 Place in greased bowl, turning to coat top. Cover; let rise in warm place until double—about 1 hour.

5 Punch down dough. Divide dough in half. Make a 6 x 10-inch rectangle.

6 Combine in small bowl the brown sugar, nuts, and cinnamon. Brush dough with melted butter. Sprinkle half of nut mixture on the rectangle. Roll up jelly-roll style. Pinch seams and ends. Place on greased baking sheet toward one side. This is the handle.

7 Make two 4 x 5-inch rectangles. Brush one with melted butter. Sprinkle remaining nut mixture on top of it. Place second rectangle on top of first rectangle. Pinch edges of the two together. Place this doubled rectangle against one end of the handle.

8 Cover; let rise for 30 minutes. Bake in a preheated 375°F oven 25–35 minutes or until done. Cool on wire rack.

Frosting

Chocolate Confectioners' Icing
(p. 208)

Confectioners' Icing (p. 208)

9 Mix icings. Use Chocolate Confectioners' Icing for the handle. Use Confectioners' Icing for the head. If desired, decorate the head with cherries.

Martha Washington Fan Coffee Cake

In the time of Martha Washington, a fan was necessary to a lady's deportment on social occasions. The handling of a fan, it is said, amounted to a language in itself. Mrs. Washington had an extraordinary number of fans, and this tasty coffee cake is a worthy reminder of them. Yields 1 coffee cake.

Ingredients

2–2½ cups	flour
3 tablespoons	sugar
½ teaspoon	salt
⅓ cup	nonfat dry milk
½ tablespoon	active dry yeast
6 tablespoons	unsalted butter, softened
½ cup	hot water (120°–130°F)
1	egg
	filling (your choice)
	unsalted butter, melted
	Confectioners' Icing (p. 208)

Preparation

1 Combine 1½ cups flour, sugar, salt, dry milk, yeast, and softened butter. Add hot water to the dry ingredients and mix well.

2 Add egg and enough remaining flour to make a soft dough. Mix thoroughly.

3 Knead on lightly floured surface until smooth—about 10 minutes.

4 Place in greased bowl, turning to coat top. Cover; let rise in warm place until double—about 1 hour.

5 Prepare a filling. (See Fillings section in Chapter 20.) Punch dough down. Roll into 5 x 18-inch rectangle.

6 Brush melted butter down ⅔ the length of the dough. Sprinkle filling on the butter-covered dough. Fold unbuttered third of dough over center third. Fold again over remaining third, forming 3 layers in all. Pinch together edges and ends. Place on greased baking sheet. Using scissors, make cuts ⅔ of the way into dough at 1-inch intervals. Turn each cut section on its side so that the filling shows. Pinch ends into points. Curve slightly into fan shape.

7 Cover; let rise until double—about 45 minutes.

8 Bake in a preheated 350°F oven about 45 minutes or until done. Cool on wire rack. Frost with Confectioners' Icing.

Chapter 7

Easter Season*

*E*aster, with its associations of hope and rebirth, highlights the Christian year. Most of all, of course, the holiday commemorates the resurrection of Jesus. But Easter also marks the joyous beginning of spring, as its name (after the Teutonic goddess of spring, believed to have been Austron) indicates. The symbolism of Eastertime reflects this background—in bunnies, chicks, eggs, new clothes—and special foods.

*H*oliday breads gladden Easter celebrations around the world. Many such breads originated in the early days of Christianity or even in pagan times. The serving and eating of these breads are among our most ancient customs.

*S*ome of the most interesting breads celebrate phases of the Easter season. Thus in this chapter you will find Shrove Tuesday buns for the Tuesday before Lent and hot cross buns as well as caraway bread for Good Friday.

*W*hen for Easter Day itself the bread recipes given here—coming from more that ten different countries—illustrate the diversity of Easter celebrations. Try them not only for Easter but at any time you want to enjoy superb bread.

*Including Shrove Tuesday and Good Friday breads.

Shrove Tuesday Buns

The day before Ash Wednesday is called Shrove Tuesday. People customarily confessed on this day and were called shrove or shriven as a result—thus the name. Shrove Tuesday concluded the prelenten carnival in many countries. (Mardi Gras is one.)

Ingredients

3–3½ cups	flour
¼ cup	sugar
½ teaspoon	salt
1 tablespoon	active dry yeast
1 teaspoon	ground cardamom
¾ cup	milk
6 tablespoons	unsalted butter
1	egg
	confectioners' sugar

Preparation

1 Combine 2 cups flour, sugar, salt, yeast, and cardamom in a mixing bowl.

2 Heat milk and butter to hot (120°F–130°F). Add milk mixture to dry ingredients. Mix thoroughly.

3 Add egg and enough remaining flour to make a soft dough.

4 Knead on lightly floured surface until smooth—about 10 minutes.

5 Punch down dough. Shape dough into 12-inch rope and cut into 1-inch pieces. Shape these into smooth round buns.

6 Place on greased baking sheet. Let rise until double—about 30 minutes.

7 Bake in a preheated 400°F oven 10–15 minutes or until done. Cool on wire rack.

8 When cool, slice top off each bun and scoop out center with a fork, leaving a shell ¼- to ½-inch thick. Set crumbs aside for filling.

These cream-filled buns are a Swedish delicacy for this day, but the buns deserve to be more widely enjoyed. My family raves over them. Yields 12 buns.

9 Make filling: Mix reserved crumbs, chopped nuts, confectioners' sugar, light cream, and vanilla or walnut extract.

10 Spoon filling into buns. Add a heaping spoonful of whipped cream to each. Put tops back on and sprinkle with confectioners' sugar.

Filling

¾ cup	finely chopped nuts
¾ cup	confectioners' sugar
1 cup	light cream
½ teaspoon	vanilla or walnut extract
1 cup	heavy cream, whipped

Polish Shrove Doughnuts

Filled with jam or preserves, these doughnuts are a traditional Shrove Tuesday delicacy in Poland. You'll find them an irresistible treat. Yields 12 doughnuts.

Ingredients

2½–3½ cups	flour
1 tablespoon	active dry yeast
½ teaspoon	lemon peel
¼ teaspoon	mace
¼ cup	water
½ cup	milk
1 tablespoon	sugar
¼ teaspoon	salt
2 tablespoons	unsalted butter
¼ cup	light rum
3	egg yolks
	jam or preserves
	egg white for brushing
	vegetable oil for deep frying
	confectioners' sugar

Preparation

1 Combine 2 cups flour, yeast, lemon peel, and mace in mixing bowl. Heat water, milk, sugar, salt, and butter to hot (120°–130°F).

2 Add milk mixture, rum, and egg yolks to dry ingredients. Mix thoroughly.

3 Add enough remaining flour to form a soft dough. Knead on lightly floured surface until smooth—about 10 minutes.

4 Place in greased bowl, turning to coat top. Cover; let rise in warm place until double—about 1 hour.

5 Punch down dough. Roll out dough ¼ inch thick. Cut dough into circles, using 2½-inch cutter.* Place 1 teaspoon jam or preserves in center half of each circle. Brush edge with egg white. Place a plain circle on top.

6 Pinch edges to seal. Place on greased baking sheet. Cover; let rise until double—about 30 minutes.

7 Heat vegetable oil to 375°F. Carefully drop 2 to 4 doughnuts into hot oil. Fry until golden brown on both sides.

8 Remove with slotted spoon and drain on paper towels. While still warm, coat with confectioners' sugar. (You can dust doughnuts by shaking them in a lunch-size paper bag together with confectioners' sugar.)

*If you don't have a round cutter, make one by cutting both ends off a tuna can.

Hot Cross Buns I

The Friday before Easter receives its name ironically, as being the opposite of good. One of the most ancient customs associated with this solemn holiday is that of eating hot cross buns. In my experience these buns never fail to please—everyone loves a hot cross bun!

Ingredients

2¾–3½ cups	flour
¼ cup	sugar
½ teaspoon	salt
1 teaspoon	ground cinnamon
1 tablespoon	active dry yeast
½ cup	milk
3 tablespoons	unsalted butter
1	egg
⅓ cup	currants
½ cup	chopped mixed candied fruit
	Confectioners' Icing (p. 208)

Preparation

1 Combine 2 cups flour, sugar, salt, cinnamon, and yeast in mixing bowl. Mix thoroughly.

2 Heat milk and butter to hot (120°–130°F). Add to dry ingredients and mix thoroughly.

3 Add egg, currants, candied fruit, and enough remaining flour to form a soft dough.

4 Knead on lightly floured surface until smooth—about 10 minutes. Place in greased bowl, turning to coat top.

5 Cover; let rise in warm place until double—about 1 hour.

6 Punch down dough. Shape into 9 balls. Place in greased 9 x 9-inch pan. Make glaze and brush on buns.

7 Cover; let rise until double—about 45 minutes.

8 Bake in a preheated 350°F oven about 25 minutes or until done. Cool on wire rack.

In the first recipe, the buns are baked in a pan and come out attached to one another (the more common way). In the second recipe, buns are baked separate from one another. The first recipe makes 9 buns, the second, 12.

Glaze

1	egg yolk
2 tablespoons	water

9 Make Confectioners' Icing. Drizzle icing from spoon over each bun (lengthwise and crosswise), forming crosses.

On Making Crosses

There are several ways of making the cross on a hot cross bun:

1 Apply Confectioners' Icing on buns after baking.

2 With scissors, snip cross pattern on top of shaped buns before rising.

3 Apply flour-and-water paste cross after rising but before baking.

4 Make cross by using uncooked dough, and place on risen bun.

5 Make a cross on risen dough out of candied peel.

Hot Cross Buns II

Ingredients

1 tablespoon	active dry yeast
¼ cup	warm water (105°–115°F)
3½– 4 cups	flour
¼ cup	sugar
3 tablespoons	unsalted butter, melted
1	egg
½ cup	warm milk (105°–115°F)
½ teaspoon	salt
¼ teaspoon	grated nutmeg
¼ teaspoon	ground cloves
¼ cup	chopped candied orange peel
⅓ cup	dark raisins
	Confectioners' Icing (p. 208)

Glaze

1	egg yolk
1 tablespoon	water

Preparation

1 Dissolve yeast in warm water. Set aside for 5 minutes.

2 Combine 2 cups flour, sugar, melted butter, egg, and warm milk. Mix thoroughly.

3 Add salt, nutmeg, cloves, and yeast mixture. Mix thoroughly.

4 Knead in orange peel, raisins, and enough remaining flour to make a soft dough. Knead until smooth—about 10 minutes.

5 Place in greased bowl, turning to coat top. Cover; let rise in warm place until double—about 1 hour.

6 Punch down dough. Shape into balls of equal size.

7 Place on greased baking sheet. Brush with melted butter. Cover; let rise in warm place until double—about 30–45 minutes.

8 Make glaze and brush on loaf. If desired, use scissors to cut a cross. Bake in a preheated 350°F oven about 20–30 minutes or until done.

9 Cool on wire rack. Frost with Confectioners' Icing, making a cross on top of each bun.

(For alternative ways of making cross, see note at end of the previous recipe.)

Sourdough Hot Cross Buns

Here's one for sourdough lovers! A sourdough fan myself, I particularly like this recipe because it gives a new twist to an old tradition. Yields 12 buns.

Ingredients

½ tablespoon	active dry yeast
¼ cup	warm water (105°–115°F)
1½–2 cups	flour
¼ cup	warm milk (105°–115°F)
1 cup	sourdough starter (p. 12)
2 tablespoons	sugar
¼ teaspoon	salt
2 tablespoons	unsalted butter, softened
½ teaspoon	vanilla extract
⅓ cup	chopped red and green candied cherries
¼ cup	golden raisins
	Confectioners' Icing (p. 208)

Preparation

1 Dissolve yeast in warm water. Set aside for 5 minutes. Combine 1 cup flour, milk, sourdough starter, sugar, salt, butter, vanilla, and yeast mixture in mixing bowl.

2 Add cherries, raisins, and enough remaining flour to make a soft dough. Knead on lightly floured surface until smooth—about 10 minutes.

3 Place in greased bowl, turning to coat top. Cover; let rise in warm place until double—about 1 hour.

4 Punch down dough. Divide into 12 equal pieces. Shape into balls. Place on greased baking sheet.

5 Cover; let rise in warm place until double—about 30 minutes. Bake in a preheated 400°F oven 15–20 minutes or until done.

6 Cool on wire rack. Make crosses on top of buns with Confectioners' Icing.

Hot Cross Bread

Here's another intriguing and tasty variation on hot cross buns. This fruited loaf, handsomely adorned with one large cross, is quicker to make than the buns—and good to eat. Yields 1 loaf.

Ingredients

⅓ cup	milk
2 tablespoons	unsalted butter
¼ teaspoon	salt
2 tablespoons	sugar
1½–2 cups	flour
½ tablespoon	active dry yeast
1	egg
½ cup	dark raisins
¼ cup	chopped mixed candied fruit
	Confectioners' Icing (p. 208)

Preparation

1 Heat milk, butter, salt, and sugar to hot (120°–130°F). Combine 1 cup flour and yeast in mixing bowl. Add milk mixture to flour and mix thoroughly.

2 Add egg, raisins, candied fruit, and enough remaining flour to make a soft dough.

3 Knead on lightly floured surface until smooth—about 10 minutes. Place in greased bowl, turning to coat top.

4 Cover; let rise in warm place until double—about 1 hour.

5 Punch down dough. Shape into a ball. Place on greased baking sheet. Cut a 2-inch-long, ¼-inch-deep cross on top of loaf. (Can also be shaped as a loaf and baked in greased 8½ x 4½-inch loaf pan.)

6 Cover; let rise until double—about 45 minutes. Bake in a preheated 350°F oven about 30–40 minutes or until done.

7 Cool on wire rack. Frost with Confectioners' Icing.

Good Friday Bread

For something unusual, try this caraway bread, a Good Friday tradition in southwest England. Yields 1 loaf.

Ingredients

½ tablespoon	active dry yeast
1 cup	warm water (105°–115°F)
4–4½ cups	flour
3 tablespoons	sugar
1 teaspoon	salt
2 tablespoons	unsalted butter, softened
2 teaspoons	caraway seeds
	milk

Preparation

1 Dissolve yeast in warm water. Set aside for 5 minutes. Combine 2 cups flour, sugar, salt, butter, and caraway seeds in mixing bowl. Mix thoroughly.

2 Add yeast mixture, and gradually add remaining flour to form a soft dough. Knead on lightly floured surface until smooth—about 10 minutes.

3 Place in greased bowl, turning to coat top. Cover; let rise in warm place until double—about 1 hour.

4 Punch down dough. Shape into large round loaf. Place on greased baking sheet. Brush top of dough with milk.

5 Cover; let rise in warm place until double—about 45 minutes or until done.

6 Bake in a preheated 400°F oven 40–50 minutes. Cool on wire rack.

Babka (BOB-kah) I

The word babka means "grandmother" in Polish, and its normally fluted sides resemble a woman's skirt. The first of the two versions here of this Polish classic is extremely (and traditionally) rich. The second, just as tasty, is less rich. Each yields 1 cake.

Ingredients

⅔ cup	warm milk (105°–115°F)
3½–4½ cups	flour
1 tablespoon	active dry yeast
¼ cup	warm water (105°–115°F)
7	egg yolks
½ cup	sugar
½ teaspoon	salt
1 teaspoon	vanilla extract
½ teaspoon	almond extract
4 tablespoons	unsalted butter, melted
¼ cup	chopped candied citron
¼ cup	chopped candied orange peel
¼ cup	chopped candied lemon peel
½ cup	chopped almonds
¼ cup	golden raisins
	whole almonds
	fine dry bread crumbs

Preparation

1 Combine warm milk and ½ cup flour. Beat thoroughly and cool. Dissolve yeast in warm water. Set aside for 5 minutes.

2 Combine milk mixture and yeast mixture. Mix thoroughly. Cover; let rise in warm place until double—about 20 minutes.

3 Using electric mixer at medium speed, beat egg yolks and sugar about 5 minutes. Add salt, extracts, and butter. Mix.

4 Add enough remaining flour to make a soft dough. Knead on lightly floured surface until smooth—about 10 minutes.

5 Put in greased bowl, turning to coat top. Cover; let rise in warm place until double—about 1 hour.

6 Knead in candied citron, peels, chopped almonds, and raisins for about 10 minutes. Cover with inverted bowl; let rest for 20 minutes.

7 Punch down dough. Grease a 6-cup Bundt pan. Press whole almonds around bottom and side of pan. Dust lightly with bread crumbs.

8 Put dough in prepared pan. Dough should fill about half of the pan. Cover; let rise in warm place until double—about 45–60 minutes.

9 Bake in a preheated 350°F oven 1 hour or until done. Cool in pan about 15 minutes; then cool on wire rack.

Babka II

Ingredients

1 tablespoon	active dry yeast
¼ cup	warm water (105°–115°F)
1 stick	unsalted butter, melted
½ cup	sugar
4	egg yolks
3½–4 cups	flour
½ teaspoon	salt
1 teaspoon	vanilla extract
1 teaspoon	rum flavoring
¾ cup	warm milk (105°–115°F)
	fine dry bread crumbs
	confectioners' sugar

Preparation

1 Dissolve yeast in warm water. Set aside for 5 minutes. Cream butter and sugar in mixing bowl. Add egg yolks, 1½ cups flour, and mix thoroughly.

2 Add yeast mixture, salt, vanilla, and rum flavoring.

3 Add milk and enough remaining flour to form a soft dough.

4 Knead on lightly floured surface until smooth—about 10 minutes. Place in greased bowl, turning to coat top.

5 Cover; let rise in warm place until double—about 1 hour.

6 Punch down dough. Generously grease 10-inch Bundt pan. Lightly coat pan with bread crumbs. Put dough into prepared pan.

7 Cover; let rise in warm place until double—about 45 minutes.

8 Bake in a preheated 350°F oven 45 minutes or until done.

9 Cool in pan on wire rack 10 minutes. Then remove from pan. Cool on rack. Sprinkle with confectioners' sugar before serving.

• **Note:** You may prefer to make babka in a round or a braided loaf and bake on a baking sheet. Or you can bake babka in a 2-quart soufflé dish.

Czechoslovakian Easter Cake

This great bread splendidly celebrates Easter. Whatever your ethnic origins, it will enhance your holiday table. Make a round loaf as described, or braid if you prefer with four, five, or six ropes. Yields 1 loaf.

Ingredients

1 tablespoon	active dry yeast
⅓ cup	warm water (105°–115°F)
2–2½ cups	flour
3 tablespoons	sugar
½ teaspoon	salt
1 teaspoon	grated lemon peel
1 stick	unsalted butter, softened
¼ teaspoon	ground mace
⅓ cup	warm milk (105°–115°F)
2	eggs
½ cup	golden raisins
½ cup	chopped almonds
	sliced almonds

Glaze

1	egg, beaten with 1 tablespoon water

Preparation

1 Dissolve yeast in warm water. Set aside for 5 minutes. Combine 1½ cups flour, sugar, salt, lemon peel, butter, and mace in mixing bowl.

2 Add yeast mixture, milk, and eggs. Mix thoroughly. Add enough remaining flour to form a soft dough.

3 Knead in raisins and chopped almonds on lightly floured surface until smooth—about 10 minutes. Place in greased bowl, turning to coat top.

4 Cover; let rise in warm place until double—about 1 hour.

5 Punch down dough. Knead the dough on lightly floured surface. Shape into round loaf.

6 Place on greased baking sheet. Let rise in warm place until double—about 30 minutes.

7 Make glaze and brush on loaf. Using a sharp knife, cut a cross on top of loaf. Sprinkle with sliced almonds. Bake in a preheated 350°F oven 45–50 minutes or until done. Cool on wire rack.

Kulich (Koo-LEECH)

This bread still highlights Easter in the Soviet Union. People bring a loaf to church for the priest to bless and then serve it as part of dessert following Easter dinner. Point out when you serve it that the frosted top represents a church dome with snow on it. Yields 1 loaf.

Ingredients

1 tablespoon	active dry yeast
¼ cup	warm water (105°–115°F)
½ cup	warm milk (105°–115°F)
⅓ cup	sugar
6 tablespoons	unsalted butter, melted
½ teaspoon	vanilla extract
¼ teaspoon	almond extract
½ teaspoon	ground cardamom
½ teaspoon	salt
1½ tablespoons	grated lemon peel
2–3 cups	flour
2	beaten eggs
½ cup	toasted slivered almonds
½ cup	chopped candied mixed fruit

Icing

¼ cup	confectioners' sugar
½ tablespoon	lemon juice

Preparation

1 Dissolve yeast in warm water. Set aside for 5 minutes. Combine warm milk, sugar, butter, vanilla, almond extract, cardamom, salt, and lemon peel in a large bowl.

2 Add 1½ cups flour, yeast mixture, and eggs. Mix thoroughly. Add almonds and candied fruit.

3 Add enough remaining flour to make a soft dough.

4 Knead on lightly floured surface until smooth—about 10 minutes.

5 Place in greased bowl, turning to coat top. Cover; let rise in warm place until double—about 1½ hours.

6 Punch down dough. Shape into a ball; try to get a nicely rounded top. Place in well-greased 1-pound coffee can. Cover; let rise in warm place until double—about 45 minutes.

7 Bake in a preheated 350°F oven 35–40 minutes or until done. Cool on wire rack.

8 Mix thoroughly confectioners' sugar and lemon juice. Spoon icing over top of kulich, allowing to drip down sides. If you wish to be traditional, use candied fruit to form letters "XB," standing for "Christ is risen."

• **Note:** You may bake kulich in a well-greased 1½-quart casserole.

Paska (PAH-ska)

Ukrainians like to place Paska in a basket with decorated eggs and take the arrangement to church for the priest's blessing. Afterward they eat the food as an Easter breakfast. You'll enjoy this as an Easter bread that's properly festive but not too heavy. Yields 1 loaf.

Ingredients

1	egg
1	egg yolk
2½–3½ cups	flour
¼ cup	sugar
½ teaspoon	salt
1 tablespoon	active dry yeast
1 teaspoon	grated lemon peel
1 teaspoon	grated orange peel
½ teaspoon	vanilla extract
¼ cup	golden raisins
½ cup	milk
4 tablespoons	unsalted butter
	melted butter, if desired

Preparation

1 Beat egg and egg yolk until fluffy and light. Add 2 cups flour, sugar, salt, yeast, lemon peel, orange peel, vanilla, and raisins. Mix thoroughly.

2 Heat milk and butter to hot (120°–130°F). Add to flour mixture. Mix thoroughly.

3 Add enough remaining flour to form a soft dough. Knead on lightly floured surface until smooth—about 10 minutes.

4 Place in greased bowl, turning to coat top. Cover; let rise in warm place until double—about 1 hour.

5 Punch down dough. Set aside a little of the dough to be used as decoration on top of the loaf. Shape the rest into a ball.

6 Place in greased cake pan 3 inches deep and 6 inches across or 1 quart soufflé dish. Make cross of remaining piece of dough; place on top of loaf.

7 Cover; let rise in warm place until double—about 30 minutes.

8 Bake in a preheated 350°F oven 45–60 minutes or until done. Cool on wire rack. While still warm, brush with melted butter if desired.

Romanian Easter Braid

The delicious walnut filling of this bread helps make it a Romanian classic. Serve it as a snack or with Easter dinner. Yields 1 loaf.

Ingredients

3½–4 cups	flour
½ tablespoon	active dry yeast
½ teaspoon	grated lemon or orange peel
⅔ cup	milk
4 tablespoons	unsalted butter
¼ cup	sugar
½ teaspoon	salt
2	eggs

Filling

⅓ cup	water
⅓ cup	sugar
1 cup	finely ground almonds
½ teaspoon	grated lemon or orange peel
½ teaspoon	ground cinnamon

Glaze

1	egg, beaten with 2 tablespoons milk

Preparation

1 Combine 2 cups flour, yeast, and lemon or orange peel in mixing bowl. Heat milk, butter, sugar, and salt to hot (120°–130°F).

2 Add milk mixture and eggs to dry ingredients. Mix thoroughly.

3 Add enough remaining flour to form a soft dough. Knead on lightly floured surface until smooth—about 10 minutes.

4 Place in greased bowl, turning to coat top. Cover; let rise in warm place until double—about 1 hour.

5 Punch down dough. Divide dough into 3 equal pieces. Roll each into 7 x 16-inch rectangle.

6 Use ⅓ of filling on each rectangle; roll up jelly-roll style. Seal seam and ends. Braid; place on greased baking sheet.

7 Cover; let rise in warm place until double—about 30 minutes. Make glaze and brush on loaf.

8 Bake in a preheated 350°F oven for 40 minutes or until done. Cool on wire rack.

German Yeast Crown

In Germany, this anise-flavored crown is served on Easter morning filled with colored eggs. Yields 1 crown.

Ingredients

3½–4 cups	flour
1 tablespoon	active dry yeast
½ teaspoon	grated lemon peel
½ teaspoon	aniseeds
¾ cup	milk
1 stick	unsalted butter
¼ cup	sugar
¼ teaspoon	salt
2	eggs
½ cup	golden raisins

Glaze

	sugar
	sliced almonds
1	egg, beaten with 1 tablespoon water

Preparation

1 Combine 1½ cups flour, yeast, lemon peel, and aniseeds in mixing bowl.

2 Heat milk, butter, sugar, and salt to hot (120°–130°F). Add milk mixture to flour mixture. Mix thoroughly.

3 Add eggs, raisins, and enough remaining flour to make a soft dough.

4 Knead on lightly floured surface until smooth—about 10 minutes. Place in greased bowl, turning to coat top.

5 Let rise in warm place until double—about 1 hour.

6 Punch down dough. Divide dough into 3 equal pieces. Roll into 22-inch ropes. Braid. Place on greased baking sheet and shape into a circle.

7 Make glaze and brush on loaf. Sprinkle lightly with sugar; place almonds on top.

8 Let rise in warm place—about 10 minutes. Don't worry about any cracks in the top surface after it is baked.

9 Bake in a preheated 350°F oven for 30 minutes or until done. Cool on wire rack.

• **Note:** When serving at Easter breakfast, place colored hard-cooked eggs in center of crown.

Viennese Easter Braid

You can reproduce the culinary splendor of Vienna in your own kitchen with this braid wreathed around an Easter egg. Yields 1 loaf.

Ingredients

2 tablespoons	golden raisins
2 tablespoons	chopped candied citron
2 tablespoons	rum
2½–3 cups	flour
½ tablespoon	active dry yeast
¼ cup	sugar
½ teaspoon	salt
4 tablespoons	unsalted butter
½ cup	milk
2	eggs
3½ tablespoons	slivered almonds
1	white uncooked egg
	confectioners' sugar, if desired

Glaze

1	egg, beaten with 1 tablespoon water

Preparation

1 Soak raisins and citron in rum in small bowl for 30 minutes.

2 Combine 1½ cups flour and yeast in mixing bowl. Heat sugar, salt, butter, and milk to hot (120°–130°F).

3 Combine flour mixture, milk mixture, and eggs. Mix thoroughly.

4 Add 2 tablespoons almonds, soaked fruit, and enough remaining flour to make a soft dough. Knead on lightly floured surface until smooth—about 10 minutes.

5 Place in greased bowl, turning to coat top. Cover; let rise in warm place until double—about 1½ hours.

6 Punch down dough. Let rise until double—about 1 hour. (This is the second rising.)

7 Punch down dough. Divide in 3 equal pieces. Braid; place on greased baking sheet.

8 Make glaze and brush on loaf. Place uncooked egg in center of braid. Sprinkle with remaining almonds.

9 Cover. Let rise in warm place until double—about 30 minutes.

10 Bake in a preheated 350°F oven for 45 minutes or until done. Cool on wire rack. If desired, dust with confectioners' sugar.

• **Note:** You may make this as a round loaf or braid with 4, 5, or 6 ropes.

Paaschbrood (PAHS-brode)—Dutch Easter Bread

This rich bread, filled with raisins and candied lemon peel, is a favorite in Holland for Easter breakfast. It has all the wholesome richness we associate with Dutch cuisine. Yields 1 loaf.

Ingredients

½ cup	milk
4 tablespoons	unsalted butter
2 tablespoons	sugar
½ teaspoon	salt
2½–3 cups	flour
½ tablespoon	active dry yeast
1	egg
½ cup	golden raisins
¼ cup	chopped candied lemon peel
	Confectioners' Icing (p. 208)

Preparation

1 Heat milk, butter, sugar, and salt to hot (120°–130°F). Combine 1 cup flour and yeast in mixing bowl.

2 Add milk mixture to dry ingredients. Mix thoroughly. Add egg and enough remaining flour to make a soft dough.

3 Knead on lightly floured surface until smooth—about 10 minutes. Place in greased bowl, turning to coat top.

4 Cover; let rise in warm place until double—about 1 hour.

5 Punch down dough. Place on lightly floured surface and knead in raisins and lemon peel. Cover with inverted bowl; let rest for 20 minutes.

6 Shape and place in greased 9 x 5-inch loaf pan. Cover; let rise until double—about 1 hour.

7 Bake in a preheated 375°F oven for 35–45 minutes or until done. Cool on wire rack.

8 Frost with Confectioners' Icing.

Pääsiäisleipä (PASS-ee-ice-lay-pa)—Finnish Easter Bread

This rich Finnish bread is traditionally baked in a milking pail to symbolize abundance. Use a coffee can as an alternative. You cut the loaf by dividing it into quarters and then slicing off triangular pieces. It's especially tasty with cheese. Yields 1 loaf.

Ingredients

1 tablespoon	active dry yeast
¼ cup	warm water (105°–115°F)
2–2½ cups	white flour
¾ cup	light cream
2	egg yolks
⅓ cup	sugar
1 stick	unsalted butter
½ teaspoon	salt
1 teaspoon	ground cardamom
1 teaspoon	grated lemon peel
1 teaspoon	grated orange peel
½ cup	golden raisins
½ cup	chopped almonds
½ cup	warm milk (105°–115°F)
1 cup	rye flour
	melted butter

Preparation

1 Dissolve yeast in warm water. Set aside for 5 minutes. Combine 1 cup white flour, yeast mixture, and cream in mixing bowl. Mix thoroughly.

2 Cover; let rise in warm place until double—about 30 minutes.

3 Add egg yolks, sugar, butter, salt, cardamom, lemon peel, orange peel, raisins, and almonds to the mixture above. Mix thoroughly.

4 Stir in milk and rye flour. Add enough remaining white flour to form a soft dough. Knead on lightly floured surface until smooth— about 10 minutes. Place in greased bowl, turning to coat top.

5 Cover; let rise in warm place until double—about 1 hour.

6 Punch down dough. Make a ball. Place dough, rounded side up, in well-greased 2-pound coffee can. Let rise until dough *just comes to the top of the can.*

7 Bake in a preheated 350°F oven about 1 hour or until done. While hot, brush top of loaf with butter. Let cool in the can for about 15 minutes. Then remove from can and cool on wire rack.

Brazilian Fruit Bread

A rich bread popular at Eastertime in Brazil, this will give a Latin flavor to your Easter. Note the elegant touch of an egg decorated with a cross. Yields 1 loaf.

Ingredients

½ tablespoon	active dry yeast
2 tablespoons	warm water (105°–115°F)
½ cup	milk
4 tablespoons	unsalted butter
3 tablespoons	sugar
¼ teaspoon	salt
2½–3 cups	flour
½ teaspoon	ground cinnamon
¼ teaspoon	ground allspice
¼ teaspoon	grated nutmeg
¼ cup	golden raisins
¼ cup	chopped dried apricots
¼ cup	chopped Brazil nuts
1	egg
1	colored uncooked egg
1 tablespoon	heavy cream
	sugar

Preparation

1 Dissolve yeast in warm water. Set aside for 5 minutes. Heat milk, butter, sugar, and salt to warm (105°–115°F).

2 Combine 1½ cups flour, cinnamon, allspice, nutmeg, yeast mixture, and milk mixture in mixing bowl. Mix thoroughly. Mix 1 cup flour, raisins, apricots, and Brazil nuts in separate bowl. Mix thoroughly.

3 Add egg and fruit mixture to batter. Mix thoroughly.

4 Add enough remaining flour to form a soft dough. Knead on lightly floured surface until smooth—about 10 minutes.

5 Place in greased bowl, turning to coat top. Cover; let rise in warm place until double—about 1 hour.

6 Punch down dough. Set aside a 2½-inch ball of dough. Shape dough into loaf and place in 4 x 8-inch greased pan. Cover; let rise until double—about 30 minutes.

7 Center a colored, uncooked egg on top of loaf.* Roll out remaining dough into two ropes; make a cross over egg.

8 Brush top with cream, and sprinkle on some sugar. Bake in a preheated 400°F oven about 30–40 minutes or until done. Cool on wire rack.

• **Note:** If you don't have heavy cream, make an egg glaze and brush top.

* You should use Easter egg dye—not ordinary food coloring, which may run.

Italian Cheese Easter Bread

How about a cheese-flavored Easter bread? This bread, permeated with cheese, is a favorite in northern Italy—and one you may enjoy as a change of pace from sweeter breads. Yields 1 loaf.

Ingredients

3–3½ cups	flour
¾ cup	grated Parmesan cheese
¼ cup	grated American cheese if desired
½ teaspoon	salt
¼ teaspoon	freshly ground black pepper
1 stick	unsalted butter
¼ cup	milk
1 tablespoon	active dry yeast
¼ cup	warm water (105°–115°F)
3 tablespoons	olive oil
3	eggs, beaten

Preparation

1 Combine 2 cups flour, cheeses, salt, and pepper in large mixing bowl. Heat butter and milk to warm (105°–115°F).

2 Dissolve yeast in warm water. Set aside for 5 minutes.

3 Add milk mixture, yeast mixture, oil, and eggs to flour and cheese. Mix thoroughly.

4 Add enough remaining flour to form a soft dough. Knead on lightly floured surface until smooth.

5 Place in greased bowl, turning to coat top. Cover; let rise in warm place until double—about 1½ hours.

6 Punch down dough. Make loaf and place in a greased 9 x 5-inch pan.

7 Cover; let rise in warm place until double—about 45 minutes.

8 Bake in a preheated 375°F oven for about 40 minutes or until done. Cool on wire rack.

• **Note:** Watch this bread because it browns quickly.

Cupid's Coffee Cake, page 40 ▲

Lombardy Easter Bread

Lemon is what gives character to this superb Italian bread.
Yields 1 loaf.

Ingredients

3½–4 cups	flour
1 tablespoon	active dry yeast
½ teaspoon	salt
⅓ cup	sugar
½ teaspoon	grated nutmeg
¼ teaspoon	ground allspice
½ teaspoon	greated lemon peel
⅔ cup	milk
3 tablespoons	unsalted butter
3	eggs
⅓ cup	chopped candied lemon peel

Glaze

1	egg, beaten with 1 tablespoon water

Preparation

1 Combine 2 cups flour, yeast, salt, sugar, nutmeg, allspice, and lemon peel in mixing bowl. Heat milk and butter to hot (120°–130°F).

2 Add milk mixture and eggs to dry ingredients. Mix thoroughly.

3 Add enough remaining flour to form a soft dough. Knead in candied lemon peel.

4 Knead on lightly floured surface until smooth—about 10 minutes. Place in greased bowl, turning to coat top.

5 Cover; let rise in warm place until double—about 1 hour. Punch down dough.

6 Divide dough into 4 equal pieces. Make 4 balls; place in greased 10-inch cake pan. Cover; let rise in warm place until double—about 30 minutes.

7 Make glaze and brush on loaf. Bake in a preheated 350°F oven for 45 minutes or until done. Cool on wire rack.

Easter Dove

This bread, in Italian called La Colomba di Pasqua, makes a tasty and highly ornamental addition to an Easter celebration. Yields 1 dove.

Ingredients

½ tablespoon	active dry yeast
2 tablespoons	warm water (105°–115°F)
6 tablespoons	unsalted butter, softened
¼ cup	sugar
1 tablespoon	grated lemon peel
1 teaspoon	vanilla extract
¼ teaspoon	almond extract
¼ teaspoon	salt
3–4 cups	flour
2	eggs
2	egg yolks
⅓ cup	warm milk (105°–115°F)
16	whole almonds
1	egg white, beaten
	sugar

Preparation

1 Dissolve yeast in warm water. Set aside for 5 minutes.

2 Mix together butter, sugar, lemon peel, vanilla, almond extract, and salt. Add 2 cups flour, eggs, and egg yolks. Mix thoroughly.

3 Mix in milk and dissolved yeast. Add enough remaining flour to make a soft dough.

4 Knead on lightly floured surface until smooth—about 10 minutes.

5 Place in greased bowl, turning to coat top. Cover; let rise in warm place until double—about 1 hour.

6 Punch down dough. Knead on lightly floured surface. Divide dough in half.

7 Make an oval about 4 x 7 inches for the wings. Place slightly above middle of narrow dimension of greased baking sheet. Roll out a triangle about 12 inches high and 6 inches across the bottom. Lay triangle over oval. Twist narrow end over for head. Pinch to form beak. Then fold wide end in opposite direction for tail. Make eight 2-inch cuts for feathers, and spread tail into fan shape. (See drawings, page 71.)

The dove shape of this bread commemorates the battle of Legnano in 1176, when a pair of doves landed before the Milanese army—an occurrence taken to be a sign of divine favor leading to victory.

Almond Paste Topping

3 ounces	almond paste (p. 215)
1	egg white, slightly beaten
3 tablespoons	sugar

8 Make Almond Paste Topping. Cream together almond paste, egg white, and sugar. Spread thickly on wings. If desired, press almonds into wings.

9 Let rise in warm place until slightly puffy—about 20 minutes. *Don't let it rise too much or it will lose its shape during baking.*

10 Brush rest of dove with beaten egg white. Sprinkle generously with sugar.

11 Bake in a preheated 325°F oven about 45 minutes or until done. If browning too much, cover with foil.

12 Cool on wire rack.

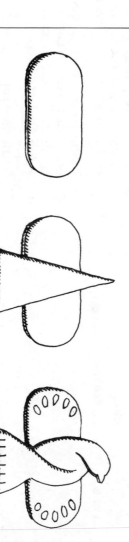

• **Note:** You may prefer to frost the entire dove and put whole almonds on the wings.

Italian Easter Basket

This (flat) basket of bread is a fine Italian Easter tradition that deserves to be adopted widely. At the top of the basket is a row of eggs, making it one of the loveliest Easter breads.
Yields 1 basket.

Ingredients

2–2½ cups	flour
½ tablespoon	active dry yeast
¼ cup	sugar
¼ teaspoon	salt
½ teaspoon	grated lemon peel
¼ teaspoon	crushed aniseeds
½ cup	milk
2 tablespoons	unsalted butter
2	eggs
4 or 5	colored uncooked eggs

Preparation

1 Combine 2 cups flour, yeast, sugar, salt, lemon peel, and aniseeds in mixing bowl.

2 Heat milk and butter to hot (120°–130°F). Add milk mixture and eggs to dry ingredients. Mix thoroughly.

3 Add enough remaining flour to make a soft dough. Knead on lightly floured surface until smooth—about 10 minutes.

4 Place in greased bowl, turning to coat top. Cover; let rise in warm place until double—about 1 hour.

5 Punch down dough. Divide dough into 3 equal pieces.

6 See drawing, page 73. Using first third of dough, make a base for basket—top 9 inches across, sides 5 inches long, and bottom 5 inches across. (▽) Place on greased baking sheet.

7 Using second third of dough, make 18–22 pencil-thin ropes. Place one rope corner to corner across the base. Place other ropes parallel to first, ½ inch apart. Next weave ropes across for a lattice effect.

8 Trim each rope, leaving ½-inch overlap of base. Carefully tuck ends under basket base.

9 With remaining dough, form additional ropes ½ inch thick as follows: Make and braid together three 20-inch-long ropes. Place in a semicircle as handle for basket and twist ends. Make and twist

Glaze

1 egg white, beaten with 1 tablespoon water

10 together two 10-inch-long ropes. Place this 1 inch below top of basket base for trim. Cut ends, leaving ½-inch overlap. Tuck ends under base, using knife.

Make two 6-inch-long ropes. Twist; place at bottom of basket for trim. Cut ends with ½-inch overlap. Tuck ends under base, using knife.

11 Place colored uncooked eggs in basket at top.* Curve heavy foil strips on both sides of handle to preserve shape.

12 Make glaze and brush on loaf. Bake in a preheated 350°F oven for 30 minutes or until done. Cool on wire rack.

*Use Easter egg dye—not ordinary food coloring, which may run.

Portuguese Sweet Bread

This bread from Portugal is plainer than many other Easter breads, which allows its delicate lemon flavor to come through. Note that the egg placed in it symbolizes the resurrection—a tradition that reaches far back into antiquity. Yields 1 loaf.

Ingredients

½ tablespoon	active dry yeast
2 tablespoons	warm water (105°–115°F)
¼ cup	milk
4 tablespoons	unsalted butter
⅓ cup	sugar
½ teaspoon	salt
2½–3 cups	flour
2	eggs
½ teaspoon	grated lemon peel
½ tablespoon	lemon juice
1	uncooked egg

Preparation

1 Dissolve yeast in warm water. Set aside for 5 minutes. Heat milk, butter, sugar, and salt to warm (105°–115°F).

2 Combine 2 cups flour, milk mixture, yeast mixture, eggs, lemon peel, and lemon juice. Mix thoroughly.

3 Add enough remaining flour to make a soft dough. Knead on lightly floured surface until smooth—about 10 minutes.

4 Place in greased bowl, turning to coat top. Cover; let rise in warm place until double—about 1 hour.

5 Punch down dough. Set aside a ball of dough about 1½ inches in diameter. Shape rest of dough into a round loaf, and place in greased 8-inch round cake pan.

6 Cover; let rise in warm place until almost double—about 30–45 minutes.

7 Place an uncooked egg in the middle of the loaf. (In Portugal, these eggs are not colored.) Press down gently to keep in place. Make 2 ropes about 9 inches long, and form a cross over egg.

8 Bake in a preheated 375°F oven about 45 minutes or until done. Cool on wire rack.

Pan de Feria (PAHN day FAY-ree-ah)

In Mexico, this festival bread is made in half a dozen or so small loaves—each with an Easter greeting or a person's name. You can personalize your loaves in this way. Yields 1 loaf.

Ingredients

1 tablespoon	active dry yeast
1/3 cup	warm water (105°–115°F)
2½–3 cups	flour
1 teaspoon	grated lemon peel
2/3 cup	milk
4 tablespoons	unsalted butter
1 tablespoon	sugar
½ teaspoon	salt
1	egg

Glaze

1	egg, beaten with 1 tablespoon water

Preparation

1 Dissolve yeast in warm water. Set aside for 5 minutes. Combine 1½ cups flour and lemon peel in mixing bowl.

2 Heat milk, butter, sugar, and salt to warm (105°–115°F). Add yeast mixture, milk mixture, and egg to dry ingredients. Mix thoroughly.

3 Add enough remaining flour to form a soft dough. Knead on lightly floured surface until smooth—about 10 minutes.

4 Place in greased bowl, turning to coat top. Cover; let rise in warm place until double—about 1 hour.

5 Punch down dough. Shape into a ball. Place on greased baking sheet. (This makes a large loaf—you may want to make 2 smaller loaves.) Flatten slightly.*

6 Cover; let rise in warm place until double—about 35–45 minutes. Cut a cross on top of loaf. Make glaze and brush on loaf.

7 Bake in a preheated 350°F oven 1 hour for large loaf, 30 minutes for smaller. Cool on wire rack.

*To make 6 or 8 small loaves, Mexican style: Shape into ball; flatten slightly. Mix 1/3 cup flour, 1/3 cup soft butter, and 2 teaspoons warm water together until smooth. Put writing tip in a pastry bag and fill with mixture. Write Easter greetings or names on each loaf. Sprinkle sesame seeds around edge.

Greek Trinity Bread

The Greeks make their Trinity Bread in the shape of a three-leaf clover. You will find that it serves as a striking Easter centerpiece, especially with a colored cloth bow placed on top. Yields 1 loaf.

Ingredients

½ tablespoon	active dry yeast
2 tablespoons	warm water (105°–115°F)
¼ cup	milk
3 tablespoons	sugar
¼ teaspoon	salt
4 tablespoons	unsalted butter
1½–2 cups	flour
½ teaspoon	crushed aniseeds
1	egg
¼ cup	golden raisins
Glaze	
1	egg, beaten with 1 tablespoon water

Preparation

1 Dissolve yeast in warm water. Set aside for 5 minutes. Heat milk, sugar, salt, and butter to warm (105°–115°F).

2 Combine 1½ cups flour, yeast mixture, milk mixture, aniseeds, and egg in large bowl. Mix thoroughly.

3 Add raisins and enough remaining flour to form a soft dough. Knead on lightly floured surface until smooth—about 10 minutes.

4 Place in greased bowl, turning to coat top. Cover; let rise in warm place until double—about 1 hour.

5 Punch down dough. Cut dough into 3 equal pieces; shape into smooth balls. Place about 1 inch apart on greased baking sheet in a cloverleaf shape. Press lightly with hand.

6 Cover; let rise until almost double—about 30 minutes. Make glaze and brush on loaf.

7 Bake in a preheated 350°F oven about 30 minutes or until done. Cool on wire rack. When ready to serve, place a big cloth bow on the center if desired.

Lambropsomo (lam-BROP-so-mo)—Easter Bread

In Greek, Easter is lambri and bread is psomi—hence the name of this Easter delicacy. With dyed eggs in the shape of a cross, the bread has a spectacular appearance. Yields 1 loaf.

Ingredients

⅓ cup	milk
6 tablespoons	unsalted butter
⅓ cup	sugar
½ teaspoon	salt
1 tablespoon	active dry yeast
⅓ cup	warm water (105°–115°F)
3–3½ cups	flour
2	eggs
¼ teaspoon	ground cinnamon
¼ teaspoon	grated nutmeg
¼ teaspoon	ground allspice
5	uncooked eggs, dyed red
1	egg white
	sesame seeds

- **Note:** To make a braid, divide dough into 3 ropes. Place uncooked egg in center of braid. You should use Easter egg dye—not ordinary food coloring, which may run.

Preparation

1 Heat milk, butter, sugar, and salt to warm (105°–115°F).

2 Dissolve yeast in warm water. Set aside for 5 minutes. Combine 2 cups flour, milk mixture, and eggs. Mix thoroughly.

3 Add cinnamon, nutmeg, and allspice. Add enough remaining flour to form a soft dough.

4 Knead on floured surface until smooth—about 10 minutes.

5 Place in greased bowl, turning to coat top. Cover; let rise in warm place until double—about 1 hour.

6 Punch down dough. Place on lightly floured surface. Set aside ⅛ of the dough for decoration. Shape remaining dough into round loaf. Place on greased baking sheet.

7 Place 1 dyed uncooked egg in center and the other 4 dyed eggs around the edge as tips of a cross.

8 Divide remaining dough into 10 parts. Roll into 5-inch strips. Arrange 2 strips in a cross shape over each egg. Press ends down to keep eggs in place.

9 Cover; let rise in warm place until double—about 45–60 minutes. Brush with egg white and sprinkle with sesame seeds.

10 Bake in a preheated 375°F oven 30–40 minutes or until done. Cool on wire rack.

Tsoureki (tsu-RAY-kee)—Easter Twist I

Here is a fabulous braided bread the Greeks bake for Easter. Try the first recipe for a plainer loaf, the second for a rich one. One taste of either, and you'll know why tsoureki is a classic. Both recipes yield 1 loaf.

Ingredients

⅓ cup	milk
3 tablespoons	unsalted butter
2–2½ cups	flour
¼ cup	sugar
¼ teaspoon	salt
½ tablespoon	active dry yeast
¾ teaspoon	grated lemon peel
¼ teaspoon	aniseeds
1	egg
5	uncooked eggs, dyed scarlet
1	egg white, slightly beaten

Preparation

1 Heat milk and butter to hot (120°–130°F). Combine 1½ cups flour, sugar, salt, and yeast in mixing bowl. Add milk mixture and mix thoroughly.

2 Add lemon peel, aniseeds, and egg. Mix thoroughly.

3 Add enough remaining flour to make a soft dough. Knead on lightly floured surface until smooth—about 10 minutes.

4 Place in greased bowl, turning to coat top. Cover; let rise in warm place until double—about 1 hour.

5 Punch down dough.

6 For a wreath, divide into 3 equal pieces and braid, forming into a wreath.

7 Place wreath on greased baking sheet. Place dyed eggs around the wreath, equally apart.*

8 Cover; let rise in warm place until double—about 30 minutes.

9 Brush egg white on top of dough. Bake in preheated 350°F oven about 30 minutes or until done.

• **Note:** For a round loaf, make a ball out of the dough. Place in 9-inch cake pan. For a rectangular loaf, roll up dough and place in a greased 5 x 9-inch loaf pan.

*You should use Easter egg dye—not ordinary food coloring, which may run.

78

Tsoureki—Easter Twist II

Ingredients

½ tablespoon	active dry yeast
¼ cup plus 2 tablespoons	warm water (105°–115°F)
1 tablespoon	anise liqueur
¼ teaspoon	ground cinnamon
¼ teaspoon	aniseeds
½ teaspoon	grated orange peel
¼ cup	milk
3 tablespoons	unsalted butter
¼ teaspoon	salt
¼ cup	sugar
1½–2 cups	flour
1	egg
3 tablespoons	sliced almonds
1	egg yolk
	coarsely chopped almonds

Preparation

1 Dissolve yeast in 2 tablespoons warm water. Set aside for 5 minutes. Heat ¼ cup water, liqueur, cinnamon, aniseeds, and orange peel to warm (105°–115°F).

2 In another saucepan, heat milk, butter, salt, and sugar to warm (105°–115°F).

3 Combine 1 cup flour, yeast mixture, spice mixture, milk mixture, and egg in bowl. Mix thoroughly.

4 Add sliced almonds and enough remaining flour to make a soft dough. Knead on lightly floured surface until smooth—about 10 minutes.

5 Punch down dough. Divide dough in half; roll into 2 equal-size ropes. Twist loosely.

6 Place on greased baking sheet. Cover; let rise until almost double—about 30 minutes.

7 Brush loaf with egg yolk. Sprinkle with almonds. Bake in a pre-heated 350°F oven 40–55 minutes or until done. Cool on wire rack.

Bunny Curlicues

*Here's a twist that especially charms children. The bunnies in
this recipe are a delightful touch on an Easter table.
Yields 12 bunnies.*

Ingredients

½ tablespoon	active dry yeast
2 tablespoons	warm water (105°–115°F)
⅓ cup	milk
2 tablespoons	sugar
¼ teaspoon	salt
4 tablespoons	unsalted butter
2–2½ cups	flour
1	egg
1 teaspoon	grated lemon peel
¼ teaspoon	ground mace
	currants
	Confectioners' Icing (p. 208), if desired

Preparation

1 Dissolve yeast in warm water. Set aside for 5 minutes. Heat milk, sugar, salt, and butter to warm (105°–115°F).

2 Add 2 cups flour, egg, lemon peel, and mace. Mix thoroughly.

3 Add enough remaining flour to make a soft dough. Knead on lightly floured surface until smooth—about 10 minutes.

4 Place in greased bowl, turning to coat top. Cover; let rise in warm place until double—about 1 hour.

5 Punch down dough. Divide into 12 equal pieces. From each piece roll an 18-inch strip of dough. Out of this, coil up a 10-inch strip for body, a 5-inch strip for head, and two 1-inch strips (make pointed) for ears. Roll remaining 1-inch strip into a ball for tail. Put in 1 currant for eye (rabbit is portrayed in side view).

6 Place on greased baking sheet. Cover; put in warm place until double—about 30 minutes.

7 Bake in a preheated 375°F oven 10–15 minutes or until done. Cool on wire rack.

8 If desired, frost with Confectioners' Icing.

Easter Chicks

Here's another Easter bread with a distinctive shape. Place the chicks around the Easter table and watch everyone's eyes sparkle. Yields 12 chicks.

Ingredients

1 tablespoon	active dry yeast
¼ cup	warm water (105°–115°F)
3–4 cups	flour
pinch	powdered saffron
⅓ cup	sugar
1	egg
½ cup	evaporated milk, undiluted
6 tablespoons	unsalted butter
¼ teaspoon	salt
	dark raisins
	slivered almonds
	beaten egg

Preparation

1 Dissolve yeast in warm water. Set aside for 5 minutes.

2 Combine 2½ cups flour, saffron, sugar, egg, evaporated milk, butter, and salt. Mix thoroughly.

3 Add enough remaining flour to make a soft dough. Knead on lightly floured surface until smooth—about 10 minutes.

4 Place in greased bowl, turning to coat top. Cover; let rise in warm place until double—about 1 hour. Punch down dough.

5 Divide dough into 12 equal pieces. Roll each piece into a rope 14 inches long and about ½ inch thick. Tie each rope into loose knot. Leave one end slightly shorter than the other.

6 Put 2 inches apart on greased baking sheet. For the head, pinch the short end of each knot. Press down tail end, and make several cuts in it with scissors. Insert raisins into dough for the eyes and an almond sliver for the beak.

7 Let dough rise until double—about 20 minutes. Brush each chick with beaten egg. Bake in a preheated 400°F oven 15 minutes or until done.

8 Cool on wire rack.

Easter Braid

A colored egg in the center of this cardamom-flavored braid gives it an especially dressy appearance. Directions indicate a three-rope braid, but use four, five, or six ropes if you prefer (see pp. 7–8). Yields 1 loaf.

Ingredients

½ tablespoon	active dry yeast
2 tablespoons	warm water (105°–115°F)
¼ cup	milk
2 tablespoons	sugar
2 tablespoons	unsalted butter
¼ teaspoon	salt
1½–2 cups	flour
½ teaspoon	ground cardamom
1	egg
1	uncooked egg, dyed red
	milk
	sugar

Preparation

1 Dissolve yeast in warm water. Set aside for 5 minutes. Heat milk, sugar, butter, and salt to warm (105°–115°F).

2 Combine 1½ cups flour, yeast mixture, milk mixture, and cardamom. Mix thoroughly.

3 Add egg and enough remaining flour to make a soft dough. Knead on lightly floured surface until smooth—about 10 minutes.

4 Place in greased bowl, turning to coat top. Cover; let rise in warm place until double—about 45–60 minutes.

5 Punch down dough. Divide dough into 3 equal pieces. Make 14-inch ropes, and braid. Place on greased baking sheet. Gently place colored egg in braid.*

6 Cover; let rise until double—about 30 minutes.

7 Brush loaf with milk, and sprinkle with sugar. Bake in a preheated 350°F oven 40 minutes or until done. Cool on wire rack.

*You should use Easter egg dye—not ordinary food coloring, which may run.

Chapter 8

Purim

*F*ew holidays are more jolly than the Jewish festival of Purim. The story behind this holiday is important for the full appreciation of one of its delicacies—the bread called hamantash or, in the plural, hamantashen.

*C*oming about a month before Passover, in February or March, Purim celebrates the deliverance of Jews in ancient Persia. The King of Persia at that time is said to have had a high official called Haman who hated Jews. So influenced by Haman was the king that he ordered the seizing of Jewish property and the slaughter of all Jews on a certain date. But Esther, the queen, was secretly Jewish herself. With courage and ingenuity she foiled Haman and persuaded the king to spare the Jews.

*N*ow Jews celebrate Purim with a service in which parts of the Book of Esther are read, and the congregation sets up a good-humored din at each mention of Haman's name. During parties afterward, among the traditional treats are hamantashen, or "Haman's pockets." This bread receives its name from a similarity between its triangular shape and Haman's pocket or hat.

Hamantashen (HAH-mun-tahsh-en)

You don't have to be Jewish or wait for Purim to savor this bread. Vary your "Haman's Pockets" with the four fruit fillings described below. Yields 15.

Ingredients

½ tablespoon	active dry yeast
2 tablespoons	warm water (105°–115°F)
½ cup	milk
⅓ cup	sugar
½ teaspoon	salt
4 tablespoons	unsalted butter
2½–3 cups	flour
1	egg

Glaze

1	egg yolk, beaten with 1 tablespoon water

Fillings

Lemon-Poppy Seed

6 ounces	canned poppy seed filling
½ teaspoon	grated lemon peel
½ tablespoon	lemon juice

Preparation

1 Dissolve yeast in warm water. Set aside for 5 minutes. Heat milk, sugar, salt, and butter to warm (105°–115°F).

2 Put in mixing bowl. Add 2 cups flour, yeast mixture, and egg. Mix thoroughly.

3 Add enough remaining flour to make a soft dough.

4 Knead on lightly floured surface until smooth—about 10 minutes. Place in greased bowl, turning to coat top.

5 Cover; let rise in warm place until double—about 1 hour.

6 Punch down dough. Roll into 12 x 17-inch rectangle. Cut into 4-inch circles.

7 Make a filling (see below), and place it in center of each circle. Moisten edges. Fold sides up to form a triangle and pinch together.

8 Place on greased baking sheet. Cover; let rise until double—about 30 minutes.

9 Make glaze and brush on loaf. Bake in a preheated 350°F oven 15–20 minutes or until done.

10 Cool on wire rack.

• Combine poppy seed filling, lemon peel, and lemon juice. In each circle place about ½ tablespoon filling.

Prune

1 cup	unpitted prunes
1/4 cup	sugar
1/4 cup	ground walnuts
1/2 teaspoon	grated lemon peel
1/2 tablespoon	lemon juice

- Rinse prunes. Simmer for 15 minutes in saucepan filled with water to 1 inch above prunes; drain. Pit and chop prunes. Add sugar, nuts, lemon peel, and lemon juice. Mix thoroughly. Place about 1 tablespoon filling in each circle.

Plum

1 cup	plum jam
1/3 cup	chopped nuts
1/3 cup	fine dry bread crumbs

- Combine plum jam, nuts, and bread crumbs. Mix thoroughly. Place about 1/2 tablespoon filling in each circle.

Apricot

1 cup	dried apricots
2 tablespoons	sugar
2 tablespoons	honey
1/2 teaspoon	ground cinnamon
1/2 teaspoon	grated nutmeg
1 teaspoon	grated lemon or orange peel
1/4 cup	ground pecans

- Cook apricots in water until tender. Drain and chop. Add sugar, honey, cinnamon, nutmeg, lemon or orange peel, and pecans. Place about 1 tablespoon filling in each circle.

Chapter 9

St. Patrick's Day

March 17

On one day of the year Americans of many different ancestries suddenly become Irish. The general public enjoys participating in St. Patrick's Day regardless of ethnic background.

St. Patrick was born in the fourth century and dedicated his life to converting pagan Ireland to Christianity. His holy works, including the reputed elimination of snakes and toads from Ireland, have made him the island's revered patron saint.

St. Patrick's Day won early recognition in America. George Washington ordered "St. Patrick" to be the countersign on March 17, 1776, when his troops were encamped at Cambridge, Massachusetts. Public celebrations had begun in Boston earlier in that century.

Wearing green and marching in parades are obvious ways of celebrating St. Patrick's Day. But you can add magic to the occasion with a distinctive bread from this chapter.

Freckle Bread

The freckles (raisins) in this traditional Irish bread give it unusual eye appeal, along with its hearty flavor. Yields 1 loaf.

Ingredients

2–3 cups	flour
¼ cup	sugar
½ teaspoon	salt
1 tablespoon	active dry yeast
½ cup	potato water or water
4 tablespoons	unsalted butter
1	egg
2 tablespoons	mashed potatoes
½ cup	golden raisins

Preparation

1 Combine 1½ cups flour, sugar, salt, and yeast in a large bowl.

2 Combine potato water or water and butter in a saucepan. Heat to hot (120°–130°F).

3 Combine potato water mixture with dry ingredients and beat until smooth. Add egg, potatoes, raisins, and enough remaining flour to make a soft dough.

4 Knead until smooth—about 10 minutes. Place in greased bowl, turning to coat top.

5 Cover; let rise in warm place until double—about 1 hour.

6 Punch down dough. On lightly floured surface divide dough into 2 equal pieces. Form each piece into slender loaf about 9 inches long.

7 Place 2 loaves side by side in greased 5 x 9-inch pan. Cover; let rise in warm place until double—about 1 hour.

8 Bake in a preheated 350°F oven 30–40 minutes or until done. Cool on wire rack.

Shamrock Rolls

These plain, fragrant rolls, in the shape of Ireland's national emblem, make an excellent St. Patrick's Day surprise for family or friends. Yields 12 rolls.

Ingredients

2–2½ cups	flour
½ tablespoon	active dry yeast
½ teaspoon	salt
2 tablespoons	sugar
½ cup	milk
3 tablespoons	unsalted butter
2 tablespoons	water
¼ cup	mashed potatoes
1	egg

Preparation

1 Combine 1½ cups flour, yeast, salt, and sugar. Heat milk, butter, and water to hot (120°–130°F).

2 Combine milk mixture and mashed potatoes with dry ingredients.

3 Add egg and enough remaining flour to make a soft dough. Knead on lightly floured surface until smooth—about 10 minutes.

4 Place in greased bowl, turning to coat top. Cover; let rise in warm place until double—about 1 hour.

5 Punch down dough. Divide into 12 equal pieces and shape into rolls. (There are 2 ways of shaping—see below.)

6 Place on greased baking sheet, and let rise until double—about 20 minutes.

7 Bake in a preheated 375°F oven 15–25 minutes or until done. Cool on wire rack.

Two Ways of Shaping

(a) Divide each roll into 4 equal balls and place in a greased muffin pan.

(b) Make a ball and place in a greased muffin pan. With scissors dipped in flour, snip top in half; snip crosswise, making 4 points.

Irish Soda Bread

*Although no yeast is used in Irish soda bread, it's included here
as Ireland's traditional bread—a favorite snack with tea.*
Yields 1 loaf.

Ingredients

2 cups	flour
1 teaspoon	baking powder
½ teaspoon	baking soda
½ teaspoon	salt
3 tablespoons	sugar
1 tablespoon	caraway seeds
3 tablespoons	unsalted butter
⅔ cup	dark raisins
¾ cup	buttermilk
1 tablespoon	unsalted butter, melted
½ tablespoon	sugar

Preparation

1 Combine flour, baking powder, baking soda, salt, sugar, and caraway seeds in mixing bowl.

2 Cut in butter until mixture looks like coarse meal. Stir in raisins; add buttermilk gradually. Mix thoroughly.

3 Knead on lightly floured surface until smooth—about 5 minutes. Shape in a ball. Place in greased 8-inch round cake pan.

4 Cut a 4-inch cross about ⅔ through center of dough. Brush top with melted butter; sprinkle with sugar.

5 Bake in a preheated 350°F oven about 30 minutes or until a cake tester comes out clean. Cool on wire rack.

Chapter 10

St. Joseph's Day

March 19

*J*oseph, the Virgin Mary's husband, was a carpenter like Jesus. Despite the sketchy references to Joseph in the Bible, devotion to him has grown through the ages. He is recognized as a saint by the Greek Orthodox and some Episcopal Churches. The Roman Catholic Church assigns him a rank among saints second only to the Virgin Mary. March 19 is his feast day in the Roman Catholic and some Episcopal Churches; the Greek Orthodox Church observes the feast on December 26.

*S*t. Joseph's Day customs vary widely. In Italy the people of some regions have feasts while people in other regions stage festivals or parades. Italian families in the United States sometimes celebrate the day with an open house and a feast (meatless because the day falls in Lent) at which three children sit at a separate table and portray the Holy Family.

A common thread running through many of the celebrations in the United States and abroad is the serving of St. Joseph's Bread. Often shaped like a patriarch's beard, this bread is blessed by the priest—in church, out in the street during festivals, or some-times at parties in the home. In addition, participants in the feasts may receive small individual loaves of bread and lucky fava beans.

St. Joseph's Bread

Why not welcome spring with some delicious Pane di San Giuseppe, St. Joseph's bread—a fine Italian tradition? Yields 1 loaf.

Ingredients

2–3 cups	flour
½ tablespoon	active dry yeast
1 teaspoon	honey
⅔ cup	hot water (120°–130°F)
½ teaspoon	salt
2 tablespoons	unsalted butter
3 tablespoons	aniseeds
⅓ cup	golden raisins
	cornmeal

Preparation

1 Combine 1½ cups flour, yeast, honey, hot water, salt, butter, and aniseeds in a large bowl. Mix thoroughly. Add raisins.

2 Add enough remaining flour to make a soft dough.

3 Knead on lightly floured surface until smooth—about 10 minutes.

4 Place in greased bowl, turning to coat top. Cover; let rise in warm place until double—about 1 hour.

5 Punch down dough. Shape into long loaf.* (Tradition says you should point the bread to look like a patriarch's beard.) Grease baking sheet, and sprinkle with cornmeal. Place loaf on baking sheet. Cut loaf 3 or 4 times diagonally ½ inch deep.

6 Cover; let rise in warm place—about 30 minutes.

7 Spray with water. Bake in a preheated 350°F oven 30 minutes or until done. Spray 3 or 4 times during baking.

8 Cool on wire rack.

*If preferred, make 3 ropes and braid.

Chapter 11

Independence Day

July 4

*I*ndependence Day, or the Fourth of July, is the major nonreligious holiday in the United States. At first the day of celebration was expected to be July 2, the day on which the Continental Congress passed a resolution of independence in 1776. But the celebration shifted to July 4—the day Congress adopted the document of the Declaration of Independence.

*J*ohn Adams, later to be president, had the first date in mind when he wrote his wife that the anniversary should be "solemnized with pomp and parade, with shows, games and sports, guns, bells, bonfires and illuminations, from one end of this continent to the other, from this time forward, forevermore." Adams's wish has been fulfilled many times over on the Fourth. But the recipes given here add a personal tribute to public displays.

Independence Day Bread

This bread had its beginning in Philadelphia, along with the event it celebrates. Tradition says you should ice it with white frosting and surround it with a wreath of gold leaves as an emblem of victory. Yields 1 loaf.

Ingredients

2 tablespoons	chopped candied citron
2 tablespoons	golden raisins
2 tablespoons	currants
1/4 cup	brandy
3–3 1/2 cups	flour
1 tablespoon	active dry yeast
1/2 teaspoon	ground cloves
1/2 teaspoon	ground cinnamon
1/4 teaspoon	grated nutmeg
1/4 teaspoon	ground allspice
4 tablespoons	unsalted butter, softened
1/2 cup	sugar
1/2 teaspoon	salt
1/2 cup	hot water (120°–130°F)
1	egg
	Confectioners' Icing (p. 208)

1 Soak citron, raisins, and currants in brandy in a small bowl about 30 minutes.

2 Combine 1 1/2 cups flour, yeast, spices, butter, sugar, salt, and hot water in mixing bowl. Mix thoroughly.

3 Add egg, soaked fruit, and enough remaining flour to make a soft dough. Knead on lightly floured surface until smooth—about 10 minutes.

4 Place in greased bowl, turning to coat top. Cover; let rise in warm place until double—about 1 hour.

5 Punch down dough. Place in a greased 6-cup Bundt pan.

6 Cover; let rise in warm place until double—about 30 minutes.

7 Bake in a preheated 350°F oven for 45–55 minutes or until done. Cool on wire rack.

8 Frost with Confectioners' Icing.

New England Raisin Bread

New Englanders have long served this raisin bread on special occasions—including Independence Day. Yields 1 loaf.

Ingredients

½ tablespoon	active dry yeast
2 tablespoons	warm water (105°–115°F)
2–3 cups	flour
½ cup	warm milk (105°–115°F)
2 tablespoons	sugar
½ teaspoon	salt
1	egg
3 tablespoons	unsalted butter, softened
½ cup	dark raisins
½ teaspoon	grated lemon peel
	melted butter
	sugar

Preparation

1 Dissolve yeast in warm water. Set aside for 5 minutes.

2 Combine 1½ cups flour, warm milk, sugar, salt, egg, butter, raisins, grated lemon peel, and yeast mixture. Mix thoroughly.

3 Add enough remaining flour to make a soft dough. Knead on lightly floured surface until smooth—about 10 minutes.

4 Place in greased bowl, turning to coat top. Cover; let rise in warm place until double—about 1 hour.

5 Punch down dough. Shape into loaf; place in greased 9 x 5-inch bread pan.

6 Cover. Put in warm place and let rise—about 30 minutes.

7 Brush loaf with melted butter, then sprinkle with sugar.

8 Bake in a preheated 350°F oven 30–40 minutes or until done. Cool on wire rack.

Chapter 12

Halloween

The power of Halloween comes partly from its great antiquity. For thousands of years, Druids in France and the British Isles held a major festival at Halloween-time, marking the end of their summer. Called Samhain (SAH-win), this holiday was supposed to be accompanied by a near riot of supernatural creatures. Ghosts, witches, elves, and other eerie beings were thought to be abroad on the night before the festival, and numerous customs developed to appease these dangerous beings.

The Romans outlawed Druidism. Then Christianity absorbed many of the pagan customs of Samhain into All Saints Day, honoring all the saints. This substitute holiday gave rise to Halloween, or "Hallowed Evening." Yet among Celtic peoples the old traditions remained vigorous, coming to this country along with the Scots and the Irish. It is fitting that the bread in this chapter, Barmbrack, has long been served in Ireland on Halloween.

Barmbrack

In Irish, barmbrack means "speckled cake." It's a must at Halloween for those who respect the old ways. Try its magic at your celebration. Yields 1 loaf.

Ingredients

½ cup	milk
4 tablespoons	unsalted butter, softened
½ tablespoon	active dry yeast
2 tablespoons	warm water (105°–115°F)
2–3 cups	flour
½ teaspoon	salt
½ teaspoon	ground allspice
1	egg
½ cup	sugar
½ tablespoon	grated lemon peel
½ cup	currants
½ cup	golden raisins
1 tablespoon	chopped candied lemon peel
	melted butter
	sugar

Preparation

1 Heat milk and butter to warm (105°–115°F). Dissolve yeast in warm water. Set aside for 5 minutes.

2 Combine 1½ cups flour, salt, allspice, milk mixture, egg, sugar, lemon peel, and yeast mixture in large bowl. Mix thoroughly.

3 Dust the fruits with ½ cup flour before adding to dough. Add enough remaining flour to make a soft dough. Knead dough on lightly floured surface until smooth—about 10 minutes.

4 Put in greased bowl, turning to coat top. Cover; let rise in warm place until double—about 1½ hours.

5 Punch down dough. Place dough into greased 9 x 5-inch loaf pan or 1½ quart casserole. Cover; let rise again until double—about 45 minutes.

6 Bake in a preheated 350°F oven 40–45 minutes or until done.

7 Brush hot loaf with melted butter, and then sprinkle with sugar. Cool on wire rack.

Chapter 13

All Souls' Day

November 2

This holiday honors the souls of the dead—known and unknown, at rest and wandering. Food is traditionally prepared for the souls and sometimes left out for them. Even now, the faithful often go to cemeteries to make their offerings directly to the deceased.

Much of the celebration takes place on All Souls' Eve (November 1). Lights at the window in Europe are beacons for wandering souls. In Mexico, fireworks brighten the night. English girls traditionally go door to door seeking soul cakes (see recipe) with a song such as this:

> Soul! soul! for a soul cake!
> I pray, good misses, a soul cake—
> An apple or pear, a plum or a cherry,
> Any good thing to make us merry.

In Mexico, the people turn out in force for the "Day of the Dead." This is a national holiday that reflects the acceptance of death by the Mexican people. Participants flock to cemeteries, carrying flowers and other offerings, such as food. They believe the dead enjoy the food though the living eat it afterward. Mementoes of death can be seen everywhere throughout the day and even after. Candy skulls with glittering eyes, coffin-shaped pastries, toy funeral processions, skeleton marionettes, grisly masks, and jewelry embellished with death's-heads are among many examples. Most interesting for us is the special pan de muerto, or bread of the dead.

Soul Cakes

This plain bread, a tradition in England, is for All Souls' Eve. You can make it in the form of round cakes or in the shape of ghostly people. Yields 12 cakes.

Ingredients

½ tablespoon	active dry yeast
2 tablespoons	warm water (105°–115°F)
3 tablespoons	sugar
4 tablespoons	unsalted butter
¾ cup	milk
½ teaspoon	salt
2–3 cups	flour
1½ teaspoons	ground cinnamon

Preparation

1 Dissolve yeast in warm water. Set aside for 5 minutes. Heat sugar, butter, milk, and salt to warm (105°–115°).

2 Combine 1½ cups flour, cinnamon, yeast mixture, and milk mixture. Mix thoroughly.

3 Add enough remaining flour to make a soft dough. Knead on lightly floured surface until smooth—about 10 minutes.

4 Place in greased bowl, turning to coat top. Cover; let rise in warm place until double—about 1 hour.

5 Punch down dough. Divide into 12 equal pieces. (You can make a long rope and divide.)

6 Make each piece into a round bun. Place on greased baking sheet. Cover; let rise in warm place until double—about 20 minutes.

7 Brush with water. Bake in a preheated 350°F oven about 20–25 minutes or until done. Cool on wire rack.

• **Note:** In olden days these cakes were shaped like people, with raisin or currant eyes.

Paska, page 61 ▶

Bread of the Dead

The fascinating flavor of this bread—with hints of orange and aniseeds—evokes the mystery of the day it celebrates. Unforgettable. Yields 1 loaf.

Ingredients

½ tablespoon	active dry yeast
2 tablespoons	warm water (105°–115°F)
1½–2 cups	flour
½ teaspoon	crushed aniseeds
1 teaspoon	grated orange peel
¼ teaspoon	salt
3 tablespoons	sugar
1	egg
3 tablespoons	unsalted butter, melted
½ teaspoon	orange extract
	Confectioners' Icing (p. 208)
	sugar, if desired

Preparation

1 Dissolve yeast in warm water. Set aside for 5 minutes. Combine flour, aniseeds, orange peel, salt, and sugar in mixing bowl.

2 Add yeast mixture, egg, butter, and orange extract to dry ingredients. Mix thoroughly.

3 Add enough remaining flour to make a soft dough. Knead on lightly floured surface until smooth—about 10 minutes.

4 Place in greased bowl, turning to coat top. Cover; let rise in warm place until double—about 1 hour.

5 Punch down dough. Use small amount of dough to make "crossbones." (Skip crossbones if you wish.) Make a round loaf with rest of dough.

6 Place loaf on greased baking sheet. Brush water on top of loaf just where you wish crossbones to stick.

7 Cover; let rise in warm place until double—about 20 minutes. Bake in a preheated 375°F oven 30 minutes or until done. Cool on wire rack.

8 Mix thin Confectioners' Icing and brush on loaf. If desired, sprinkle sugar on crossbones.

Chapter 14
Election Day

Election Day, a legal holiday in most states, did not at first fall on the same date throughout the nation. But in 1845 Congress set the Tuesday after the first Monday in November as the day of national elections. Many states followed suit by scheduling their own elections at the same time.

Customs vary widely on Election Day. Evidence of one kind is the widespread law against the sale of retail liquor while the polls are open. Indeed, alcohol once flowed freely as some voters made their uncertain way to the polls. But other election customs have been more sedate.

Connecticut was long famed for its Old Hartford Election Cake— really a raisin bread with spices and sometimes brandy in it. Visitors to the State Capitol on Election Day received pieces. Other New England states boasted similar election "cakes." Although Election Cake dates back to the eighteenth century, it is similar to a bread traditionally eaten in Britain on Guy Fawkes Day, November 5, commemorating the unmasking of the Gunpowder Plot in 1605 to blow up Parliament.

Modern election coverage by television, with its dramatic evening-long presentation, offers a perfect opportunity to revive at home the tradition of serving this to election watchers.

Election Cake

You can make a party out of an election with the aid of this delightful raisin bread that dates back to the eighteenth century. Note that this is a batter bread and requires no kneading. Yields 1 cake.

Ingredients

1 tablespoon	active dry yeast
½ cup	warm water (105°–115°F)
2¼ cups	flour
½ teaspoon	ground cinnamon
¼ teaspoon	ground mace
¼ teaspoon	grated nutmeg
¼ teaspoon	ground cloves
½ teaspoon	salt
4 tablespoons	unsalted butter
½ cup	sugar
1	egg
¼ cup	brandy
¾ cup	golden raisins
¾ cup	chopped walnuts
	Confectioners' Icing (p. 208) with brandy or lemon juice

Preparation

1 Dissolve yeast in warm water. Set aside for 5 minutes. Combine flour, cinnamon, mace, nutmeg, cloves, and salt in mixing bowl.

2 Cream butter and sugar until light and fluffy. Add yeast mixture, egg, and brandy to dry ingredients. Mix thoroughly.

3 Add raisins and nuts. Pour into well-buttered 6-cup Bundt pan. Cover; let rise in warm place until double—about 1½ hours.

4 Bake in a preheated 350°F oven 1 hour or until done.

5 Remove from oven. Cool in pan for 10 minutes. Cool on wire rack.

6 Place on plate, and frost with Confectioners' Icing flavored with brandy or lemon juice.

Chapter 15

Thanksgiving and Harvest

Last Thursday in November

H arvest celebrations, such as Thanksgiving, are probably as old as farming itself. But the Thanksgiving bequeathed us by the Pilgrims follows a special English version—Harvest Home, a festival after the gathering of the main grain crop. This version had developed during the 1500s because celebrations earlier in the season sometimes got out of hand and disrupted the harvest.

T he Pilgrim's holiday in 1621 was a production that lasted three days and included about ninety (Indian) guests. It is clear that the Pilgrims at first regarded the gathering as more a time of Old World joy and frolic than a religious occasion. New Englanders came to cherish this tradition of the early settlers. Then in 1863 Abraham Lincoln turned this local feast of Thanksgiving into a national holiday with religious overtones.

A mericans across the land have since taken up standard Thanksgiving customs such as the serving of turkey and pumpkin pie. But too often such holiday fare comes with everyday bread. This chapter offers a solution—recipes both for Thanksgiving breads specifically and for harvest breads in general.

Cranberry Yeast Bread

Cranberries are a hallmark of Thanksgiving, and this fresh-cranberry bread will make your celebration special. Yields 1 loaf.

Ingredients

⅔ cup	fresh cranberries
¼ cup	light brown sugar, firmly packed
2 tablespoons	molasses
½ tablespoon	active dry yeast
2 tablespoons	warm water (105°–115°F)
2 tablespoons	honey
⅓ cup	warm water (105°–115°F)
½ teaspoon	salt
2 tablespoons	unsalted butter, softened
½ teaspoon	ground mace
1½–2 cups	whole wheat flour
1	egg

Glaze

1	egg, beaten with 1 tablespoon water

Preparation

1 Wash and dry cranberries. Cut in half. Mix brown sugar, molasses, and cranberries. Let stand for about 30 minutes.

2 Dissolve yeast in warm water. Set aside for 5 minutes. Combine honey, water, salt, butter, mace, and yeast mixture in bowl.

3 Add 1½ cups whole wheat flour and egg. Mix thoroughly. Add enough remaining flour to make a soft dough.

4 Knead on lightly floured surface until smooth—about 10 minutes.

5 Place in greased bowl, turning to coat top. Cover; let rise in warm place until double—about 1¼ hours.

6 Punch down dough. Shape into loaf; place in 5 x 9-inch greased loaf pan.

7 Cover; let rise in warm place until double—about 30–40 minutes. Make glaze and brush on loaf.

8 Bake in a preheated 350°F oven 45 minutes or until done. Cool on wire rack.

Thanksgiving Squash Braid

Here's something different and colorful for Thanksgiving—a bread that comes out golden inside. Its color adds a handsome touch to the festive table. Braid with three, four, five, or six ropes, as you wish. Yields 1 loaf.

Ingredients

6 ounces	frozen winter squash
1 tablespoon	active dry yeast
2 tablespoons	warm water (105°–115°F)
⅓ cup	warm milk (105°–115°F)
3 tablespoons	light brown sugar, firmly packed
4 tablespoons	unsalted butter, softened
1	egg
¼ teaspoon	salt
2–2½ cups	flour

Glaze

1	egg, beaten with 1 tablespoon water

Preparation

1 Cook squash as directed on package. Dissolve yeast in warm water. Set aside for 5 minutes.

2 Combine squash, milk, brown sugar, butter, egg, and salt in mixing bowl. Mix thoroughly.

3 Add yeast mixture and 1½ cups flour. Mix thoroughly.

4 Add enough remaining flour to make a soft dough. Knead on lightly floured surface until smooth—about 10 minutes.

5 Place in greased bowl, turning to coat top. Cover; let rise in warm place until double—about 1 hour.

6 Punch down dough. Divide into thirds. Make 3 ropes and braid. Place on greased baking sheet.

7 Cover; let rise in warm place until double—about 30 minutes.

8 Make glaze and brush on loaf. Bake in a preheated 350°F oven 30 minutes or until done. Cool on wire rack.

Harvest Sheaf

Here's a really dressy bread, shaped like a sheaf of wheat, that will add a spectacular touch to your Thanksgiving dinner.
Yields 1 sheaf.

Ingredients

½ cup	milk
1 tablespoon	unsalted butter
1 tablespoon	honey
1 tablespoon	light molasses
½ teaspoon	salt
1	large shredded wheat biscuit
2 teaspoons	active dry yeast
3 tablespoons	warm water (105°–115°F)
1 cup	whole wheat flour
2 tablespoons	wheat germ
2	eggs
2–2½ cups	white flour

Glaze

1	egg, beaten with 1 tablespoon water

Preparation

1. Heat milk, butter, honey, molasses, salt, and crumbled shredded wheat biscuit to warm (105°–115°F). Dissolve yeast in warm water. Set aside for 5 minutes.

2. Combine yeast mixture, milk mixture, and whole wheat flour. Mix thoroughly.

3. Add wheat germ, eggs, and enough white flour to make a soft dough. Knead on lightly floured surface until smooth—about 10 minutes.

4. Place in greased bowl, turning to coat top. Cover; let rise in warm place until double—about 1½ hours.

5. Punch down dough. Roll out four 5-inch ropes, eight 13-inch ropes, and eight 16-inch ropes—each rope about ½-inch thick.

6. (a) Form first layer as shown in drawing, page 109, with ropes touching, starting from center and moving left and right on a greased baking sheet. Bend ropes as you place them one at a time about a third of the way from top, at sharp angle as shown.
   (b) Form second layer on top of first, starting from center and moving left and right. Bend ropes as above while you do.
   (c) Form third layer on top of second, one rope left and the other right. Bend ropes as previously.
   (d) Twist two 5-inch ropes together and repeat with other two 5-inch ropes. Lay twists side by side across middle of sheaf, tucking ends under.

108

7 To produce ragged edges, snip with scissors along the bent portion of stalks. Make glaze and brush on loaf. Cover; let rise in warm place until double—about 30 minutes.

8 Bake in a preheated 375°F oven about 25–30 minutes or until done. Cool on wire rack.

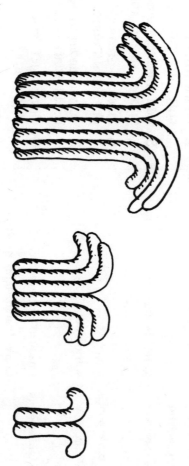

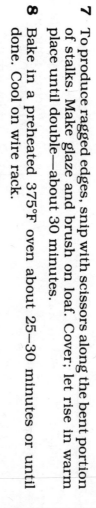

Autumn Festival Bread

This rich, hearty bread, flecked with cherries and slivered almonds, goes well with Thanksgiving dinner or as a snack in the evening. Yields 1 loaf.

Ingredients

1 tablespoon	active dry yeast
2 tablespoons	warm water (105°–115°F)
2½–3 cups	flour
½ teaspoon	salt
½ teaspoon	grated orange peel
½ cup	golden raisins
3 tablespoons	sugar
⅓ cup	warm milk (105°–115°F)
1	egg
4 tablespoons	unsalted butter, softened
	Confectioners' Icing (p. 208)
	slivered almonds
	chopped candied cherries
Glaze	
1	egg, beaten with 1 tablespoon water

Preparation

1 Dissolve yeast in warm water. Set aside for 5 minutes. Combine 1½ cups flour, salt, orange peel, raisins, and sugar in mixing bowl. Mix thoroughly.

2 Add warm milk, egg, butter, and yeast mixture to the dry ingredients. Mix thoroughly.

3 Add enough remaining flour to make a soft dough. Knead on lightly floured surface until smooth—about 10 minutes.

4 Place in greased bowl, turning to coat top. Cover; let rise in warm place until double—about 1 hour.

5 Punch down dough. Divide dough into thirds. Make 3 ropes, and braid. Place on greased baking sheet.

6 Cover; let rise in warm place until double—about 30–45 minutes.

7 Bake in a preheated 400°F oven 20 minutes. Make glaze. Remove loaf and brush with glaze. Lower oven to 325°F and continue baking 30–35 minutes or until done.

8 Cool on wire rack. Mix Confectioners' Icing, then drizzle over loaf. Sprinkle almonds and candied cherries on bread.

Chapter 16

St. Barbara's Day

December 4

St. Barbara's Day is a feast day with rich associations. Its traditional bread and other wheat foods symbolize the harvest, with overtones of death and rebirth. But the holiday's timing, in December, also links it to Christmas.

St. Barbara is said to have lived in the Middle East in the third century. Her wealthy father Dioscorus kept her secluded in a tower to protect her from harmful influences. While there, she became a Christian—to the horror of her pagan father. After remonstrating with her, Dioscorus turned her over to the governor. There followed more arguments and at last, torture. Seeing that Barbara would never forswear her faith, Dioscorus struck off his daughter's head. His reward came soon after when a bolt of lightning reduced him to ashes.

St. Barbara was patron saint of artillery and the saint invoked against thunderstorms. Christians in Syria and Lebanon long have started the Christmas season with her day, lighting candles, serving wheat-flour cakes and other delicacies, and conducting a pageant in honor of the saint.

Because of doubts about St. Barbara's authenticity, she has been dropped from the Roman Catholic Church calendar. But the delicious bread recipe that her holiday inspired should survive on its merit alone, apart from the touching legend.

St. Barbara's Bread

This spicy bread is a fitting reminder of St. Barbara, chided by her father according to legend for giving bread to the poor. Braid with three, four, five, or six ropes, as you wish. Yields 1 loaf.

Ingredients

¼ cup	milk
¼ cup	sugar
2 tablespoons	unsalted butter
¼ teaspoon	salt
½ tablespoon	active dry yeast
2 tablespoons	warm water (105°–115°F)
1	egg
½ tablespoon	lemon juice
½ teaspoon	grated nutmeg
½ teaspoon	ground allspice
½ teaspoon	ground cinnamon
1–1½ cups	flour
⅓ cup	slivered almonds
	Confectioners' Icing (p. 208)
	whole almonds, if desired

Preparation

1 Heat milk, sugar, butter, and salt to warm (105°–115°F). Dissolve yeast in warm water. Set aside for 5 minutes.

2 Combine yeast mixture, milk mixture, egg, lemon juice, nutmeg, allspice, and cinnamon. Add 1 cup flour and slivered almonds. Mix thoroughly.

3 Add enough remaining flour to make a soft dough. Knead on lightly floured surface until smooth—about 10 minutes.

4 Place in greased bowl, turning to coat top. Cover; let rise in warm place until double—about 1 hour.

5 Punch down dough. Divide into thirds. Make 3 ropes and braid. Place on greased baking sheet.

6 Let rise in warm place until almost double—about 30 minutes. Bake in a preheated 350°F oven 35–40 minutes or until done.

7 Cool on wire rack. Frost with Confectioners' Icing. If desired, decorate with almonds.

Chapter 17

St. Lucia's Day

December 13

The Christmas season in Sweden begins with St. Lucia's Day. This festival honors a Christian girl martyred in the year 304 in Syracuse, Italy.

It seems that Lucia secretly vowed as a child to dedicate her life to the Christian church. But her mother betrothed her to a pagan whom Lucia rejected. The young man retaliated by turning Lucia in to the authorities as a Christian. There followed a series of fiendish tortures that included blinding, but Lucia surmounted them all until her death by a sword thrust.

Although Lucia is a favorite in southern Europe, the Swedish people have turned her day into an especially charming festival. On the appointed day a daughter of the household is robed in a long white dress, sometimes with crimson sash and stockings. On her head she wears a whortleberry crown into which lighted candles are fitted. In this costume she goes throughout the house waking family members and serving them buns and holiday breads with coffee. The recipes given here reflect the unique appeal of this holiday.

St. Lucia Crown

The shape of this bread, in the traditional St. Lucia crown, stands for that worn by the daughter of the household. But you can make the bread in a loaf pan if you wish. Yields 1 small crown.

Ingredients

1 tablespoon	active dry yeast
¼ cup	warm water (105°–115°F)
pinch	powdered saffron
¼ cup	warm milk (105°–115°F)
2–2½ cups	flour
¼ cup	sugar
½ teaspoon	salt
1	egg
2 tablespoons	unsalted butter, softened
3 tablespoons	chopped candied citron
3 tablespoons	chopped almonds
½ tablespoon	grated lemon peel
	green and red candied cherries

Preparation

1 Dissolve yeast in warm water. Set aside for 5 minutes. Stir saffron into warm milk.

2 Combine 2 cups flour, saffron milk, sugar, salt, egg, and butter in mixing bowl. Beat until smooth. Stir in citron, almonds, and lemon peel.

3 Add enough remaining flour to make a soft dough. Knead on lightly floured surface until smooth—about 10 minutes.

4 Place in greased bowl, turning to coat top. Cover; let rise in warm place until double—about 1 hour.

5 Punch down dough. Cut off ⅓ of dough for top braid and set aside. Divide remaining dough into thirds and roll each part into 24-inch rope. Braid and shape into circle. Pinch ends together to seal. Place on greased baking sheet.

6 Divide reserved dough into thirds and roll each until 15 inches long. Braid and shape into circle. Pinch ends together to seal. Place on another greased baking sheet.

7 Cover; let rise in warm place until double—about 45 minutes.

8 Bake in a preheated 375°F oven 25 minutes or until done.

9 Cool on wire rack. When cool, make holes for 6 candles in small braid.

114

Confectioners' Icing

½ cup   confectioners' sugar

½ tablespoon   water

10 Make icing. Mix in a few more drops of water if too stiff.

11 Place small braid on large braid. Drizzle icing on braid. Decorate with cherries. Insert candles.

St. Lucia's Cats

The "cats" are curiously shaped buns traditionally served in Sweden at the dawn of St. Lucia's Day. They are great favorites with young and old. Yields 12 buns.

Ingredients

1 tablespoon	active dry yeast
¼ cup	warm water (105°–115°F)
3½–4 cups	flour
pinch	saffron
⅓ cup	sugar
1	egg
½ cup	evaporated milk, undiluted
6 tablespoons	unsalted butter
½ teaspoon	salt
	currants
	sugar

Glaze

1	egg beaten with 1 tablespoon water

(a)

(b)

(c)

Preparation

1 Dissolve yeast in warm water. Set aside for 5 minutes.

2 Combine 2 cups flour, saffron, sugar, egg, evaporated milk, butter, and salt. Mix thoroughly.

3 Add enough remaining flour to make a soft dough. Knead on lightly floured surface until smooth—about 10 minutes.

4 Place in greased bowl, turning to coat top. Cover; let rise in warm place until double—about 1 hour.

5 Punch down dough. Divide dough into 12 equal pieces. Roll each piece into 12-inch rope. Shape as shown in drawings:
(a) Cut piece of dough in half. Crisscross the 2 ropes on the baking sheet. Then curl ends in same direction.
(b) Bend rope into a V, curling ends.
(c) Cut rope in half. Arrange the 2 resulting ropes back to back, curling ends.

6 Place on greased baking sheet. Cover; let rise in warm place until double—about 20 minutes. Place a currant in each curl. Make glaze. Brush buns with glaze and sprinkle with more sugar.

7 Bake in a preheated 350°F oven about 25 minutes or until done. Cool on wire rack.

Chapter 18

Christmas Season

_W_ith Christmas, holiday breads really come into their own. The sacredness of the occasion, the centuries of tradition surrounding it, the filter of many different cultures through which the celebrations are expressed—all combine to inspire breadmakers. Furthermore, the length of the Christmas season offers an opportunity to serve a generous variety of breads. Depending on the place, Christmas celebrations extend from St. Barbara's Day to after Twelfth Night.

_O_f course, one thinks of other foods too in connection with Christmas—turkey, plum pudding, eggnog. But the breads in this chapter, from more than fifteen different countries, will deepen the holiday spirit: fruit-filled panettone from Italy and hoska from Czechoslovakia, frosted stollen from Germany, Ukrainian doughnuts, sourdough treats from the United States, and a host of others.

_T_ry these breads throughout the Christmas season—and whenever else you wish bread that creates a holiday mood.

Stollen

Stollen, the classic German Christmas bread, originally symbolized the Christ Child in swaddling clothes. No bread is more Christmasy. The first of the 2 recipes here is completely traditional, the second calls for sourdough. Yields 1 loaf.

Ingredients

1 tablespoon	active dry yeast
⅓ cup	warm water (105°–115°F)
1¾–2¼ cups	flour
¼ cup	sugar
¼ teaspoon	salt
1	egg
1	egg yolk
4 tablespoons	unsalted butter, softened
½ tablespoon	grated lemon peel
2 tablespoons	chopped candied orange peel
2 tablespoons	chopped almonds
2 tablespoons	chopped candied citron
2 tablespoons	chopped candied cherries
2 tablespoons	golden raisins
	unsalted butter, melted
	vanilla confectioners' sugar, if desired (p. 215)

Preparation

1 Dissolve yeast in warm water. Set aside for 5 minutes. Add 1½ cups flour, sugar, salt, egg, egg yolk, and butter. Mix thoroughly.

2 Add lemon peel and enough remaining flour to make a soft dough. Knead in orange peel, almonds, citron, cherries, and raisins.

3 Knead on lightly floured surface until smooth—about 10 minutes. Place in greased bowl, turning to coat top. Cover; let rise in warm place until double—about 1½ hours.

4 Punch down dough. Shape into a 7 x 10-inch oval. Brush with melted butter. Fold in half lengthwise; press only folded edge firmly.

5 Place loaf on greased baking sheet. Combine egg white and water; brush over top. Let rise in warm place until double—about 45–60 minutes.

6 Bake in a preheated 350°F oven 25–35 minutes or until done.

Glaze

1		egg white
1 tablespoon		water

Icing (optional)

¾ cup		confectioners' sugar
1 tablespoon		milk
		candied citron
		candied cherry halves

7 Cool on wire rack. Make icing, and frost. Decorate with pieces of candied citron and candied cherry halves. Or if desired, sprinkle with vanilla confectioners' sugar while warm. You may sprinkle with vanilla confectioners' sugar again before serving.

Almond Stollen (Sourdough)

Here's another version of stollen, a delightful alternative to the traditional form of this bread. Yields 1 loaf.

Ingredients

1½–2¼ cups	flour
¾ cup	sourdough starter (p. 12)
2 tablespoons	honey
1	egg
2 tablespoons	unsalted butter, melted
½ teaspoon	salt
1 teaspoon	grated lemon peel
1 cup	slivered almonds
	unsalted butter, melted
2 tablespoons	confectioners' sugar

Preparation

1 Combine 1 cup flour, sourdough, honey, egg, butter, salt, and lemon peel. Mix thoroughly.

2 Add enough remaining flour to make a soft dough. Knead on lightly floured surface until smooth—about 10 minutes.

3 Place in greased bowl, turning to coat top. Cover; let rise in warm place until double—1½ hours.

4 Punch down dough. Knead in almonds. Cover with inverted bowl for 10 minutes. Roll into a 7 x 10-inch oval. Fold in half lengthwise. Press only folded edge firmly.

5 Place stollen on greased baking sheet. Let rise in warm place until double—about 30–45 minutes.

6 Brush melted butter on top. Bake in a preheated 350°F oven 30 minutes or until done.

7 Cool on wire rack. While still warm, brush with melted butter. Then sprinkle with confectioners' sugar.

Bremen Küchen (KOO-ken)

This rich bread is a tradition in Bremen, West Germany, especially popular there with coffee. You will find it a welcome addition to a holiday party. Yields 1 loaf.

Ingredients

½ tablespoon	active dry yeast
2 tablespoons	warm water (105°–115°F)
¾ cup	milk
3 tablespoons	unsalted butter
3–4 cups	flour
2 tablespoons	sugar
½ teaspoon	salt
½ teaspoon	ground cardamom
1 teaspoon	grated lemon peel
¼ cup	golden raisins
¼ cup	dark raisins
¼ cup	currants
2 tablespoons	sliced almonds
¼ cup	chopped candied orange peel
2 tablespoons	sliced almonds, if desired
	unsalted butter, melted
	confectioners' sugar

Preparation

1 Dissolve yeast in warm water. Set aside for 5 minutes. Heat milk and butter to warm (105°–115°F).

2 Combine 2 cups flour, sugar, salt, cardamom, and lemon peel in mixing bowl. Add the yeast mixture and milk mixture to the dry ingredients. Mix thoroughly.

3 Add enough of the remaining flour to make a soft dough. On lightly floured surface knead until smooth—about 10 minutes.

4 Place in greased bowl, turning to coat top. Cover; let rise in warm place until double—about 1 hour.

5 Knead in raisins, currants, about half the almonds, and candied orange peel. Let rest; cover with inverted bowl for 10 minutes.

6 Punch down dough. Roll dough into a 12 x 15-inch rectangle. Roll up tightly from long side; seal well. Place on greased baking sheet.

7 Cover; let rise in warm place until double—about 30 minutes.

8 If desired, press remaining almonds into top of dough. Bake in a preheated 375°F oven 1 hour or until done.

9 While the bread is still hot, brush the top with melted butter. Dust top with confectioners' sugar.

10 Cool on wire rack.

Birnbrot (BEERN-broht)—Pear Bread

Enjoy this pear bread as the Swiss do, with hot chocolate.
Yields 1 loaf.

Ingredients

½ tablespoon	active dry yeast
⅓ cup	warm water (105°–115°F)
1½–2½ cups	flour
¼ teaspoon	salt
3 tablespoons	sugar
3 tablespoons	unsalted butter, softened
1	egg

Preparation

1 Dissolve yeast in warm water. Set aside for 5 minutes. Combine 1 cup flour, salt, sugar, and softened butter. Add yeast mixture and egg. Mix thoroughly.

2 Stir in enough remaining flour to make a soft dough. Knead on lightly floured surface until smooth—about 10 minutes.

3 Place in greased bowl, turning to coat top. Cover; let rise in warm place until double—about 1 hour.

4 Prepare the filling while dough is rising. Boil water in a small saucepan. Add pears, prunes, raisins, and lemon juice to water. Simmer fruit over low heat, stirring frequently, for 10 minutes or until so tender it can be mashed easily.

5 Drain fruit. Purée it in a blender. Combine the walnuts, sugar, lemon peel, cinnamon, and nutmeg with the purée. Mix thoroughly. This mixture will be thick.

6 Grease a large baking sheet. Punch down dough. Roll dough into a square 9 x 9 inches.

Filling

¾ cup	water
¾ cup	coarsely chopped dried pears
⅓ cup	pitted, coarsely chopped dried prunes
¼ cup	golden raisins
2 tablespoons	lemon juice
¼ cup	chopped walnuts
1 tablespoon	sugar
½ teaspoon	grated lemon peel
¼ teaspoon	ground cinnamon
¼ teaspoon	grated nutmeg

Glaze

1	egg, beaten with 1 tablespoon milk

7 Spread the filling on dough, covering all but a 1-inch margin. Roll the dough jelly-roll style. Place on greased baking sheet seam side down. Make glaze and brush on loaf. Let rise in warm place until double—about 30 minutes.

8 Bake in a preheated 350°F oven 30–40 minutes or until done. Cool on wire rack.

Gugelhupf (GOO-gul-hupf)

The name of this great bread comes from the words for "monk's hood yeast." To many Austrians Gugelhupf (also spelled Kugelhupf) means Christmas. Yields 1 cake.

Ingredients

½ tablespoon	active dry yeast
¼ cup	warm water (105°–115°F)
2–3 cups	flour
¼ cup	warm milk (105°–115°F)
½ cup	sugar
1 stick	unsalted butter
½ teaspoon	salt
2	eggs
⅓ cup	golden raisins
½ tablespoon	grated lemon peel
¼ cup	very finely chopped almonds
10	whole almonds

Preparation

1 Dissolve yeast in warm water. Set aside for 5 minutes.

2 Combine 1½ cups flour, milk, sugar, butter, salt, and eggs with yeast mixture in large bowl. Mix thoroughly.

3 Stir in raisins, lemon peel, and enough remaining flour to make a soft dough.

4 Knead on lightly floured surface until smooth—about 10 minutes.

5 Place the dough in lightly greased bowl, turning to coat top. Cover; let rise in warm place until double—about 1 hour.

6 Grease the side and bottom of 6-cup Bundt pan. Sprinkle with chopped almonds. Place whole almonds evenly in bottom of pan.

7 Punch down dough. Then carefully place in mold. Let rise until double—about 1 hour.

8 Bake in a preheated 350°F oven 45 minutes or until done.

9 Cool 10 minutes; remove from mold. Cool on wire rack.

Julbrod (YULE-brode)

This Swedish Yule bread comes in a wreath that looks as good as it tastes. I like to serve it on a candlelit table. Yields 1 wreath.

Ingredients

1 tablespoon	active dry yeast
2 tablespoons	warm water (105°–115°F)
2–2½ cups	flour
⅓ cup	warm milk (105°–115°F)
¼ teaspoon	salt
¼ cup	sugar
4 tablespoons	unsalted butter, softened
1	egg
1 teaspoon	ground cardamom
⅓ cup	golden raisins
⅓ cup	chopped candied lemon peel
⅓ cup	chopped almonds

Glaze

	confectioners' sugar
	sliced almonds
1	egg, beaten with 1 tablespoon water

Preparation

1 Dissolve yeast in warm water. Set aside for 5 minutes. Combine 1 cup flour, milk, salt, sugar, butter, egg, and cardamom in mixing bowl.

2 Mix ½ cup flour with raisins and lemon peel in a small bowl. Add chopped almonds. Mix.

3 Add raisin mixture to dough. Mix thoroughly. Add enough remaining flour to make a soft dough.

4 Knead on lightly floured surface until smooth—about 10 minutes. Place in greased bowl, turning to coat top.

5 Cover; let rise in warm place until double—about 1 hour.

6 Punch down dough. Let rise again about 45 minutes. Punch down dough.

7 Braid and shape into a wreath. Place on greased baking sheet. Make glaze and brush on loaf.

8 Let rise until double—about 30 minutes. Bake in a preheated 400°F oven 15 minutes. Lower oven temperature to 350°F and bake 25 minutes longer or until done. Cool on wire rack. Cover with confectioners' sugar and almonds.

Swedish Tea Ring

The Swedish people enjoy this delicate cake at Christmas, but—minus Christmas touches—you'll find it appropriate for any special occasion. Yields 1 ring.

Ingredients

½ tablespoon	active dry yeast
2 tablespoons	warm water (105°–115°F)
⅔ cup	milk
2 tablespoons	unsalted butter, softened
2 tablespoons	sugar
½ teaspoon	salt
3–3½ cups	flour
1	egg
	Confectioners' Icing (p. 208)
	additional candied fruit

Filling

1 tablespoon	unsalted butter, softened
1 tablespoon	sugar
½ teaspoon	grated lemon peel
3 tablespoons	ground almonds
⅓ cup	chopped mixed candied fruit

Preparation

1 Dissolve yeast in warm water. Set aside for 5 minutes. Heat milk, butter, sugar, and salt to warm (105°–115°F).

2 Combine 2 cups flour, milk mixture, yeast mixture, and egg in mixing bowl. Mix thoroughly.

3 Add enough remaining flour to make a soft dough. Knead on lightly floured surface until smooth—about 10 minutes.

4 Place in greased bowl, turning to coat top. Cover; put in warm place. Let rise until double—about 1 hour.

5 Punch down dough. Cream butter, sugar, lemon peel, and ground almonds. Mix thoroughly.

6 Roll dough into a 10 x 14-inch rectangle. Sprinkle ground almond mixture over dough. Place candied fruit on top.

7 Roll up jelly-roll style and seal edge. Form in a ring, sealed edge down, on greased baking sheet. Seal ends together. Snip with scissors from outside edge every 1½ inch. Turn cut pieces on side.

8 To keep hole round, place greased custard cup in center. (You can put a nondrip candle in the center for a Christmas touch when serving at the table.)

9 Cover; let rise until almost double—about 45 minutes. Bake in a preheated 350°F oven about 30 minutes or until done. Cool on rack.

10 Frost with icing and decorate with extra candied fruit.

Swedish Christmas Braid

The golden hue of saffron and the spiciness of cardamom in this bread help explain its popularity among the Swedish people during the Christmas season. Yields 1 loaf.

Ingredients

½ tablespoon	active dry yeast
2 tablespoons	warm water (105°–115°F)
½ cup	milk
3 tablespoons	unsalted butter
3 tablespoons	sugar
¼ teaspoon	salt
pinch	powdered saffron
1½–2 cups	flour
1	egg

Filling

1 tablespoon	sugar
½ teaspoon	ground cardamom
⅓ cup	golden raisins
⅓ cup	chopped candied lemon peel or citron
	unsalted butter, melted

Glaze

1 egg,	beaten with 1 tablespoon water

Preparation

1 Dissolve yeast in warm water. Set aside for 5 minutes. Heat milk, butter, sugar, salt, and saffron to warm (105°–115°F).

2 Combine 1 cup flour, yeast mixture, milk mixture, and egg in mixing bowl. Mix thoroughly.

3 Add enough remaining flour to make a soft dough. Knead on lightly floured surface until smooth—about 10 minutes.

4 Put in greased bowl, turning to coat top. Cover; let rise in warm place until double—about 1 hour.

5 While dough is rising, make filling. Combine sugar, cardamom, raisins, and lemon peel or citron in small bowl.

6 Punch down dough. Roll dough into a 6-inch square. Brush a strip 2 inches wide down the center with melted butter. Put filling down center.

7 With scissors, cut strips toward center 2 inches long and 1 inch wide. Alternating sides, fold strips over filling.

8 Place on greased baking sheet. Cover; let rise until double—about 30 minutes. Make glaze and brush on loaf. Bake in a preheated 400°F oven about 30–40 minutes or until done. Cool on wire rack.

Swedish Twist

Studded with cherries, shaped into a twist, this Swedish delicacy evokes the Scandinavian Christmas. Yields 1 loaf.

Ingredients

1 tablespoon	active dry yeast
⅓ cup	warm water (105°–115°F)
⅓ cup	sugar
½ teaspoon	salt
1 stick	unsalted butter
⅔ cup	milk
1 teaspoon	grated lemon peel
3–3½ cups	flour
1	egg
¼ cup	chopped candied cherries

Topping

1	egg yolk
1 teaspoon	milk
1 teaspoon	ground cinnamon
3 tablespoons	sugar
3 tablespoons	chopped almonds
	candied cherry halves

Preparation

1 Dissolve yeast in warm water. Set aside for 5 minutes.

2 Heat sugar, salt, butter, milk, and lemon peel to warm (105°–115°F). Combine 1½ cups flour, yeast mixture, and milk mixture. Mix thoroughly.

3 Add egg and enough remaining flour to make a soft dough. Knead in cherries.

4 Knead on lightly floured surface until smooth—about 10 minutes.

5 Place in greased bowl, turning to coat top. Let rise in warm place until double—about 1 hour.

6 Punch down dough. Divide dough in half; make two 18-inch ropes. Twist together. Pinch both ends, and tuck under.

7 Place on greased baking sheet. Cover. Let rise in warm place until double—about 30 minutes.

8 Combine egg yolk and milk; brush top of loaf. Combine cinnamon, sugar, and almonds. Sprinkle on top of loaf. Decorate with cherry halves. (If preferred, make confectioners' icing and frost top of loaf when cool. Decorate with candied cherries.)

9 Bake in a preheated 350°F oven for 35–45 minutes or until done. Cool on wire rack.

• **Note:** If preferred, make confectioners' icing flavored with cherry extract, with candied cherries on your topping.

Julekake (yoo-luh-KAH-kuh)

Yule cake, flavored with cardamom, is a big favorite during the holidays in Norway. An excellent bread for company at Christmas. Yields 1 loaf.

Ingredients

½ tablespoon	active dry yeast	
¼ cup	warm water (105°–115°F)	
¼ cup	milk	
4 tablespoons	unsalted butter	
½ teaspoon	salt	
1 teaspoon	ground cardamom	
2 tablespoons	sugar	
1¾–2 cups	flour	
1	egg	
½ cup	golden raisins	
⅓ cup	chopped mixed candied fruit	
1	egg white, beaten	
	Confectioners' Icing (p. 208)	
	candied cherries	

Preparation

1 Dissolve yeast in warm water. Set aside for 5 minutes. Heat milk, butter, salt, cardamom, and sugar to warm (105°–115°F).

2 Combine 1 cup flour, milk mixture, and yeast mixture. Mix thoroughly.

3 Add egg and enough remaining flour to form a soft dough. Knead on lightly floured surface until smooth—about 10 minutes.

4 Cover; let rise in warm place until double—about 1 hour.

5 Knead in raisins and candied fruit. Cover; let rest for 10 minutes.

6 Punch down dough. Grease a 1-pound coffee can. (Be sure to grease the grooves.) Shape dough into rounded loaf and place in can.

7 Place plastic cover loosely on can; let rise until double. (The top will pop off when ready.)

8 Brush top of loaf with egg white. Bake in a preheated 350°F oven 30–40 minutes or until done.

9 Cool on wire rack. Frost top with Confectioners' Icing. Decorate with candied cherries.

Kringle

Horseshoe-shaped and with a fruit or nut filling, Kringle adds to the Christmas Joy of Danish homes. Yields 1 cake.

Ingredients

3 tablespoons	unsalted butter
1½–2¼ cups	flour
½ tablespoon	active dry yeast
¼ cup	warm water (105°–115°F)
⅓ cup	warm light cream (105°–115°F)
1	egg
2 tablespoons	sugar
¼ teaspoon	salt
	sugar
	sliced almonds
	Confectioners' Icing (p. 208), if desired

Glaze

1	egg white, beaten with 1 tablespoon water

Preparation

1 Mix butter and 2 tablespoons flour until blended. Spread into a rectangle 4 x 8 inches on a sheet of waxed paper. Set on a baking sheet. Chill.

2 Dissolve yeast in warm water. Set aside for 5 minutes. Combine 1 cup flour, warm cream, yeast mixture, egg, sugar, and salt. Mix thoroughly.

3 Add enough remaining flour to make a soft dough. Knead on lightly floured surface until smooth—about 10 minutes.

4 Roll into an 8-inch square. Spread chilled butter down center third of dough, removing waxed paper. Fold dough over butter first from one side, then the other.

5 Roll into a 6 x 12-inch rectangle, then fold in thirds. (Do this 4 times altogether.) If the dough becomes too soft, chill in refrigerator.

6 Roll into a 6 x 24-inch rectangle. Make one of the fillings below and spread down the center of dough. Fold dough into thirds.

7 Place on lightly greased baking sheet and shape into a horseshoe. Flatten slightly. Cover; let rise in warm place until double—about 30–40 minutes.

8 Make glaze and brush on loaf. Sprinkle with sugar and sliced almonds. Bake in a preheated 350°F oven 25–30 minutes or until done. Cool on wire rack. Use Confectioners' Icing if desired.

Fillings

Almond Paste

2 tablespoons	unsalted butter, softened
¼ cup	light brown sugar, firmly packed
¼ cup	almond paste (p. 215)

- Cream butter, sugar, and almond paste until smooth.

Pecan

4 tablespoons	unsalted butter
½ cup	light brown sugar, firmly packed
1 cup	chopped pecans

- Cream butter and brown sugar. Mix in pecans.

Apple Pecan

½ cup	light brown sugar, firmly packed
1 cup	chopped apples
½ cup	chopped pecans

- Mix all ingredients.

Date Pecan

½ cup	light brown sugar, firmly packed
1 cup	chopped dates
½ cup	chopped pecans

- Mix all ingredients.

- **Note:** For a wreath, roll dough into three 2 x 24-inch rectangles. Make filling; spread ⅓ of it on each rectangle. Roll jelly-roll style; pinch seam and ends. Braid; make circle. Pinch ends together. Place on greased baking sheet. Bake as above.

131

Julekage (YOO-luh-KAY-yuh)

This is a Danish sourdough version of the Norwegian yule cake.
Yields 1 loaf.

Ingredients

1–2 cups	flour
¾ cup	sourdough starter (p. 12)
2 tablespoons	unsalted butter, melted
½ cup	honey
½ teaspoon	salt
1 teaspoon	ground cardamom
¼ cup	golden raisins
½ cup	chopped mixed candied fruit
¼ cup	chopped pecans
	candied cherries
	pecan halves

Icing

⅓ cup	confectioners' sugar
1 tablespoon	milk
½ teaspoon	vanilla or almond extract

Preparation

1 Combine ½ cup flour, sourdough starter, butter, honey, salt, and cardamom in a large bowl. Mix thoroughly.

2 Combine enough remaining flour to make a soft dough. Knead on lightly floured surface until smooth—about 10 minutes.

3 Place in greased bowl, turning to coat top. Cover; let rise in warm place until double—about 1 hour.

4 Punch down dough. Knead in raisins, candied fruit, and chopped pecans. Cover; let rest for 10 minutes.

5 Shape dough into a round ball and place on greased baking sheet. Cover; let rise until double—about 45 minutes.

6 Bake in a preheated 350°F oven 40 minutes or until done. Cool on wire rack.

7 Combine confectioners' sugar, milk, and vanilla or almond extract. Frost loaf; decorate with candied cherries and pecan halves.

Thanksgiving Squash Braid, page 107 ▶

Jolakaka (YOE-la-kah-ka)

This Icelandic form of the yule cake is a cardamom-scented version of the Scandinavian delicacy. If you make this in a coffee can (one of two suggested ways), turn on side and place a candle in the center. Then frost and decorate with candied fruit for a striking centerpiece. Yields 1 or 2 loaves.

Ingredients

¾ cup	milk
4 tablespoons	unsalted butter
⅓ cup	sugar
¼ teaspoon	salt
2½–3¼ cups	flour
½ tablespoon	active dry yeast
½ teaspoon	ground cardamom
1	egg
⅓ cup	golden raisins
¼ cup	chopped candied lemon peel
¼ cup	slivered almonds
	Confectioners' Icing (p. 208), if desired

Preparation

1 Heat milk, butter, sugar, and salt to hot (120°–130°F). Combine 1½ cups flour, yeast, and cardamom in mixing bowl.

2 Add milk mixture to dry ingredients. Mix thoroughly.

3 Add egg and enough remaining flour to make a soft dough. On lightly floured surface, knead in raisins, lemon peel, and almonds.

4 Knead until smooth—about 10 minutes. Place in greased bowl, turning to coat top. Cover; let rise in warm place until double—about 1½ hours.

5 Punch down dough. Shape and place in a 9 x 5-inch loaf pan or two 1-pound coffee cans.

6 Cover; let rise until double—about 1 hour.

7 Bake in a preheated 375°F oven about 45–55 minutes or until done. Cool on wire rack.

8 If desired, frost with Confectioners' Icing.

Viipuri (VEE-pur-ee)

Finns love these pretzel-shaped delicacies, often filled with Christmas cookies. A different and delightful holiday bread. Yields 1 twist.

Ingredients

⅔ cup	milk
¼ cup	sugar
2 tablespoons	unsalted butter
½ teaspoon	salt
2–2½ cups	flour
½ tablespoon	active dry yeast
½ teaspoon	ground cardamom
½ teaspoon	grated nutmeg
1	egg

Glaze

1	egg, beaten with 1 tablespoon water

Preparation

1 Heat milk, sugar, butter, and salt to hot (120°–130°F). Combine 1½ cups flour, yeast, cardamom, and nutmeg.

2 Add milk mixture to dry ingredients. Mix thoroughly.

3 Add egg and enough remaining flour to make a soft dough. Knead on lightly floured surface until smooth—about 10 minutes.

4 Cover; let rise in warm place until double—about 1 hour.

5 Punch down dough. Make a 32-inch-long-rope. Shape into a huge pretzel. (Make into a circle, leaving 6-inch ends curving into center. Twist ends together; then press and tuck under top of circle.) Place on greased baking sheet.

6 Cover; let rise until almost double—about 30 minutes. Make glaze and brush on loaf. Bake in a preheated 350°F oven about 30 minutes or until done. Cool on wire rack.

Finnish Potato Rye

*Here's a hearty, dark rye that goes well with a Christmas dinner.
You'll find this plainer than most festive breads but with plenty
of character. Yields 1 loaf.*

Ingredients

1 tablespoon	active dry yeast
½ cup	warm potato water (105°–115°F)
2–2½ cups	white flour
1 cup	rye flour
1 cup	warm mashed potatoes
½ cup	light molasses
½ teaspoon	salt
2 teaspoons	caraway seeds
Glaze (optional)	
2 teaspoons	sugar
2 tablespoons	warm water

Preparation

1 Dissolve yeast in potato water. Set aside for 5 minutes.

2 Combine 1½ cups white flour, rye flour, potatoes, molasses, salt, caraway seeds, and yeast mixture. Mix thoroughly.

3 Add enough remaining white flour to make a soft dough. Knead on lightly floured surface until smooth—about 10 minutes.

4 Place in greased bowl, turning to coat top. Cover; let rise in warm place until double—about 1 hour.

5 Punch down dough. Shape loaf. Place on greased 9 x 5-inch loaf pan.

6 Cover; let rise in warm place until double—about 40 minutes.

7 Bake in a preheated 350°F oven for 45 minutes or until done. Make glaze and brush on loaf. Cool on wire rack.

Finnish Coffee Bread

Served all year long in Finland with Sunday morning coffee, this becomes a Christmas treat in the shapes described here. One of our favorites because of its cardamom flavor and handsome appearance when glazed. Yields 1 loaf.

Ingredients

½ tablespoon	active dry yeast
¼ cup	warm water (105°–115°F)
¾ cup	milk
⅓ cup	sugar
½ teaspoon	salt
½ teaspoon	ground cardamom
3½–4 cups	flour
1	egg
4 tablespoons	unsalted butter, melted
	candied cherries or sliced almonds

Glaze

1	egg, beaten with 1 tablespoon water

Preparation

1. Dissolve yeast in warm water. Set aside for 5 minutes. Heat milk, sugar, salt, and cardamom to warm (105°–115°F).

2. Combine 2 cups flour, egg, yeast mixture, milk mixture, and butter. Mix thoroughly.

3. Add enough remaining flour to make a soft dough. Knead on lightly floured surface until smooth—about 10 minutes.

4. Place in greased bowl, turning to coat top. Cover; let rise in warm place until double—about 1 hour.

5. Punch down dough. Make in one of the two following shapes.

6. (a) Divide in half. Make a flat circle 15 inches in diameter. Place on greased baking sheet. Cut off small amount of dough and make S-shaped curl. Place curl in center of circle. Divide remaining dough into 3 equal pieces. Roll each piece into 14-inch rope. Braid; make a wreath. Place wreath on circle, leaving 1-inch margin.
   (b) *Bishop's Wig*: Divide into 3 equal pieces. Roll each piece into 18-inch rope. Fold 1 rope in half. Place on greased baking sheet. Coil ends up. (See drawing.) Place next rope around this one; coil ends. Do same for the third rope.

7. Cover. Let rise in warm place until double—about 30 minutes.

8. Make glaze and brush on loaf. Garnish with cherries or sliced almonds. Bake in a preheated 375°F oven for 30–45 minutes or until done. Cool on wire rack.

Vanocka (Van-OTCH-kah)

This Czechoslovakian braid is often referred to as a "Christmas twist." But you can enjoy this great bread, as Czechs do, on other festive occasions as well. Yields 1 loaf.

Ingredients

1 tablespoon	active dry yeast
2 tablespoons	warm water (105°–115°F)
3½–4 cups	flour
½ teaspoon	salt
¼ teaspoon	ground mace
1 teaspoon	aniseeds
1 teaspoon	grated lemon peel
⅔ cup	light brown sugar, firmly packed
⅓ cup	heavy cream
⅔ cup	milk
4 tablespoons	unsalted butter, softened
2	egg yolks
⅓ cup	golden raisins
⅓ cup	sliced almonds
Glaze	
1	egg yolk
1 tablespoon	light cream

Preparation

1 Dissolve yeast in warm water. Set aside for 5 minutes. Combine 2 cups flour, salt, mace, aniseeds, lemon peel, and brown sugar in mixing bowl.

2 Heat heavy cream, milk, and butter to warm (105°–115°F). Combine cream mixture and yeast mixture with dry ingredients. Mix thoroughly.

3 Add egg yolks and enough remaining flour to make a soft dough. Knead on lightly floured surface until smooth—about 10 minutes. Place in greased bowl, turning to coat top.

4 Cover; let rise in warm place until double—about 1½ hours.

5 Punch down dough. Knead in raisins and almonds. Divide dough into 5 equal pieces and make equal ropes.

6 Using 3 ropes, braid; place on greased baking sheet. Twist the 2 remaining ropes and place on the braided loaf.*

7 Cover; let rise in warm place until double—about 45 minutes.

8 Bake in a preheated 350°F oven 45 minutes. Make glaze and brush on loaf. Continue baking another 10 minutes or until done. Cool on wire rack.

*If desired, you can shape this bread into 2 round loaves.

Hoska (HOE-ska)

This beloved Christmas braid was carried by Czech immigrants throughout this country, achieving popularity among Americans of all backgrounds. Three layers of braids make hoska an especially striking addition to any festive gathering. Yields 1 loaf.

Ingredients

1 tablespoon	active dry yeast
2 tablespoons	warm water (105°–115°F)
½ cup	milk
⅓ cup	sugar
¼ teaspoon	salt
4 tablespoons	unsalted butter, softened
3–3½ cups	flour
1	egg
3 tablespoons	golden raisins
3 tablespoons	chopped candied pineapple
3 tablespoons	chopped candied orange peel
3 tablespoons	chopped candied lemon peel
3 tablespoons	chopped almonds
	sliced almonds
Glaze	
1	egg, beaten with 1 tablespoon water

Preparation

1 Dissolve yeast in warm water. Set aside for 5 minutes. Heat milk, sugar, salt, and butter to warm (105°–115°F).

2 Combine 2 cups flour, yeast mixture, milk mixture, and egg in mixing bowl. Mix thoroughly.

3 Add raisins, pineapple, orange peel, lemon peel, and chopped almonds. Add enough remaining flour to make a soft dough.

4 Knead on lightly floured surface until smooth—about 10 minutes. Place in a greased bowl, turning to coat top. Cover; let rise in warm place until double—about 1½ hours.

5 Punch down dough. Divide dough in half; divide one of these into 3 equal pieces. Roll into ropes 16 inches long. Braid; place on a greased baking sheet. Flatten slightly. Make a ¼-inch cut down the center, leaving a 1-inch margin at both ends. Dust lightly with flour.

6 Cut ⅔ off the second portion of dough; divide into 3 equal pieces. Roll into 14-inch ropes. Braid; place on the first braid. Flatten slightly. Make a ¼-inch cut down center of second braid, leaving 2-inch margin at both ends. Dust lightly with flour.

7 Divide remaining third of dough into 3 equal pieces. Roll into 10-inch ropes. Braid; place on top of second braid. Press lightly, and secure with toothpicks around outside edge of each of top 2 braids.*

8 Cover; let rise in warm, place until double—about 30 minutes. Make glaze and brush on loaf. Allow to set 2 minutes. Brush again.

9 Decorate with sliced almonds, pressing them into dough lightly. Bake in a preheated 350°F oven for 45 minutes or until done. Cool on wire rack.

*Toothpicks prevent braids from sliding while baking.

Polish Christmas Bread

From an old family recipe, this bread makes a large,
horseshoe-shaped loaf filled with candied fruit and nuts.
Yields 1 loaf.

Ingredients

½ tablespoon	active dry yeast
¼ cup	warm water (105°–115°F)
⅓ cup	milk
4 tablespoons	unsalted butter
½ teaspoon	salt
3 tablespoons	sugar
2–2½ cups	flour
½ teaspoon	vanilla extract
1	egg
	Confectioners' Icing (p. 208)
	whole almonds

Filling

2 tablespoons	sugar
½ teaspoon	ground cinnamon
¼ teaspoon	grated lemon peel
¼ teaspoon	grated orange peel

(ingredients cont.)

Preparation

1 Dissolve yeast in warm water. Set aside for 5 minutes. Heat milk, butter, salt, and sugar to warm (105°–115°F).

2 Combine 1½ cups flour, yeast mixture, milk mixture, vanilla, and egg in mixing bowl. Mix thoroughly.

3 Add enough remaining flour to make a soft dough. Knead on lightly floured surface until smooth—about 10 minutes.

4 Place in greased bowl, turning to coat top. Cover; let rise in warm place until double—about 45 minutes.

5 Make filling by combining sugar, cinnamon, grated lemon peel, grated orange peel, candied lemon peel, candied orange peel, raisins, and slivered almonds.

6 Punch down dough. Roll into a 10 x 18-inch rectangle. Brush with melted butter.

7 Spread filling over dough, leaving 1-inch margin all around. Roll up jelly-roll style and seal edge. Shape into a horseshoe. Place on greased baking sheet.

8 Cover; let rise in warm place until double—about 45 minutes. Make glaze and brush on loaf.

¼ cup	chopped candied lemon peel
¼ cup	chopped candied orange peel
2 tablespoons	golden raisins
2 tablespoons	slivered almonds
	unsalted butter, melted

Glaze

| 1 | egg, beaten with 1 tablespoon water |

9 Bake in a preheated 375°F oven about 30 minutes or until done. Cool on wire rack. Frost with Confectioners' Icing. Decorate with almonds.

Kolach (ко-lahch)

This braid is a special favorite in Ukrainian homes on Christmas Eve, when it is placed on display with a candle during supper—and then eaten. Yields 1 loaf.

Ingredients

2 teaspoons	active dry yeast
¼ cup	warm water (105°–115°F)
¼ cup	milk
3 tablespoons	sugar
½ teaspoon	salt
2 tablespoons	unsalted butter
1½–2 cups	flour
1	egg
Glaze	
1	egg, beaten with 1 tablespoon water

Preparation

1 Dissolve yeast in warm water. Set aside for 5 minutes. Heat milk, sugar, salt, and butter to warm (105°–115°F).

2 Combine 1½ cups flour, yeast mixture, and milk mixture in mixing bowl. Mix thoroughly.

3 Add egg and enough remaining flour to make a soft dough. Knead on lightly floured surface until smooth—about 10 minutes.

4 Place in greased bowl, turning to coat top. Cover; let rise in warm place until double—about 1 hour.

5 Punch down dough. Divide into 3 equal pieces. Roll into long ropes and then braid. Make glaze and brush on loaf.

6 Place on greased baking sheet. Brush with glaze. Cover; let rise until double—about 40 minutes.

7 Bake in a preheated 350°F oven 45–55 minutes or until done. Cool on wire rack.

Ukrainian Christmas Doughnuts

A favorite on Christmas Eve among Ukrainians, these filled doughnuts are an irresistible treat. Yields 12 doughnuts.

Ingredients

¼ cup	milk
3 tablespoons	sugar
2 tablespoons	unsalted butter
½ teaspoon	salt
1–1½ cups	flour
½ tablespoon	active dry yeast
½ teaspoon	grated lemon peel
1	egg
1	egg yolk
	vegetable oil for deep frying
	Confectioners' Icing (p. 208)

Preparation

1 Heat milk, sugar, butter, and salt to hot (120°–130°F). Combine 1 cup flour, yeast, and lemon peel in mixing bowl. Mix thoroughly.

2 Combine milk mixture, yeast mixture, egg, and egg yolk. Mix thoroughly.

3 Add enough remaining flour to make a soft dough. Knead on lightly floured surface until smooth—about 10 minutes.

4 Place in greased bowl, turning to coat top. Cover; let rise in warm place until double—about 1 hour.

5 Punch down dough. Roll out dough ⅛ inch thick. Cut into 2½-inch circles. Place 1 teaspoon of desired filling (see note) on half the circles; cover with plain circles. Using water, moisten edges and press them firmly to seal.

6 Cover; let rise in warm place until double—about 30 minutes.

7 In deep hot fat (375°F), fry a few at a time—about 2 minutes on each side. Drain on paper toweling. When cool, frost with Confectioners' Icing.

- **Note:** For filling, use prune cake-and-pastry filling; or cherry cake-and-pastry filling; or pineapple cake-and-pastry filling; or others of your choice.

Hungarian Christmas Bread

Do you like poppy seeds? You'll love this Hungarian gourmet bread, with its raisin and poppy seed filling. Yields 1 loaf.

Ingredients

½ tablespoon	active dry yeast
⅓ cup	warm water (105°–115°F)
1½–2 cups	flour
1 stick	unsalted butter, softened
¼ cup	sugar
½ teaspoon	salt
½ tablespoon	grated orange or lemon peel
3 tablespoons	nonfat dry milk

Filling

½ cup	poppy seeds
½ cup	sugar
⅓ cup	dark raisins
¼ cup	milk
½ tablespoon	grated orange or lemon peel

Glaze

1	egg, beaten with 1 tablespoon water

Preparation

1 Dissolve yeast in warm water. Set aside for 5 minutes.

2 Combine 1 cup flour, butter, sugar, salt, orange or lemon peel, dry milk, and yeast mixture. Mix thoroughly.

3 Add enough remaining flour to make a soft dough. Knead on lightly floured surface until smooth—about 10 minutes.

4 Place in greased bowl, turning to coat top. Cover; let rise in warm place until double—about 1½ hours.

5 As the dough rises, prepare the filling. In a saucepan, combine poppy seeds, sugar, raisins, milk, and orange or lemon peel. Stir constantly over low heat for 10 minutes. After it thickens, remove from the heat. Cool to room temperature.

6 Punch down dough. Roll piece into a long rectangle about ¼ inch thick. Spread cooled poppy seed filling on the flat dough. Roll jelly-roll style and pinch the seams together. Place on greased baking sheet.

7 Make glaze and brush on loaf. Cover; let rise—about 30 minutes.

8 Brush again with glaze. Bake in a preheated 350°F oven 45–60 minutes or until done. Cool on wire rack.

Christopsomo (kree-STOP-so-mo)

In Greek, psomi means "bread," and the name of this recipe thus means "Christ's bread"—a fragrant and delicious celebration of Christmas. Yields 1 loaf.

Ingredients

1 tablespoon	active dry yeast
⅓ cup	warm water (105°–115°F)
⅓ cup	milk
12 tablespoons	unsalted butter, softened
½ cup	sugar
½ teaspoon	salt
1 teaspoon	crushed aniseeds
4–5 cups	flour
3	eggs
12	walnut halves or candied cherries

Glaze

1	egg, beaten with 1 tablespoon water

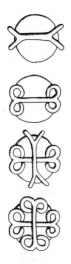

Preparation

1 Dissolve yeast in warm water. Set aside for 5 minutes. Heat milk, butter, sugar, salt, and aniseeds to warm (105°–115°F).

2 Combine 2 cups flour, yeast mixture, and milk mixture in mixing bowl. Mix thoroughly.

3 Add eggs and enough remaining flour to make a soft dough. Knead on lightly floured surface until smooth—about 10 minutes.

4 Place in a greased bowl, turning to coat top. Cover; let rise in warm place until double—about 1½ hours.

5 Punch down dough. Pinch off 2 balls of dough 3 inches in diameter. Set aside for 5 minutes. Knead remaining dough on lightly floured surface to make a smooth ball. Place on greased baking sheet; flatten dough into a 9-inch round loaf about 2 inches thick.

6 Shape each 3-inch ball into a 15-inch-long rope. Make 5-inch-long cut into each end of the ropes. Cross ropes at center of the loaf. (*Don't press down.*) Bend cut sections away from center of each rope to form circles. (See drawing.)

7 Put walnut or cherry in each circle and one in center of cross. Make glaze and brush on loaf. Cover; let rise in warm place until double—about 1 hour.

8 Bake in a preheated 350°F oven 45 minutes or until done. Cool on wire rack.

Greek Feast Bread

This bread in a 3-leaf clover shape commemorating the Trinity is a favorite at Christmas. The traditional symbolism makes this an especially charming holiday bread. Yields 1 loaf.

Ingredients

⅔ cup	milk
3 tablespoons	unsalted butter
3 tablespoons	sugar
½ teaspoon	salt
½ tablespoon	active dry yeast
3 tablespoons	warm water (105°–115°F)
3–3½ cups	flour
1	egg
1 teaspoon	grated lemon peel
½ teaspoon	ground mace
½ cup	currants

Glaze

1	egg, beaten with 1 tablespoon water

Preparation

1. Heat milk, butter, sugar, and salt to warm (105°–115°F). Dissolve yeast in warm water. Set aside for 5 minutes.

2. Combine 2 cups flour, milk mixture, yeast mixture, and egg in a mixing bowl. Mix thoroughly.

3. Add lemon peel, mace, and enough remaining flour to make a soft dough. Knead in the currants.

4. Knead on lightly floured surface until smooth—about 10 minutes. Place in greased bowl, turning to coat top.

5. Cover; let rise in warm place until double—about 1 hour.

6. Punch down dough. Divide into 3 equal pieces. Shape 3 balls. Place on greased baking sheet to form three-leaf clover. (Leave 1-inch space between balls.)

7. Cover; let rise in warm place until double—about 1 hour. Make glaze and brush on loaf.

8. Bake in a preheated 350°F oven 25–30 minutes or until done. Cool on wire rack.

Brioche Wreath

A French favorite, brioche (the traditional light bread), here assumes the form of a Christmas wreath. You'll find this a plain but very elegant bread. Yields 1 wreath.

Ingredients

1 tablespoon	active dry yeast	
¼ cup	warm water (105°–115°F)	
3–3½ cups	flour	
⅓ cup	sugar	
¼ teaspoon	salt	
4 tablespoons	unsalted butter, softened	
1	egg	
1	egg yolk	
¼ teaspoon	almond extract	
	Confectioners' Icing (p. 208)	
	whole almonds	
	candied red and green cherries	

Glaze

1	egg, beaten with 1 tablespoon water	

Preparation

1 Dissolve yeast in warm water. Set aside for 5 minutes. Combine 2 cups flour, sugar, salt, and butter in a mixing bowl. Mix thoroughly.

2 Add egg, egg yolks, almond extract, and enough remaining flour to make a soft dough.

3 Knead on lightly floured surface until smooth—about 10 minutes. Place in greased bowl, turning to coat top. Cover; let rise in warm place until double—about 1 hour.

4 Punch down dough. Shape into a ball.

5 Stretch dough to form a 4-inch hole in center. Place on greased baking sheet. Put greased custard dish in hole to hold shape.

6 Let rise in warm place until double—about 30 minutes. Make glaze and brush on loaf. Bake in a preheated 350°F oven 35–45 minutes or until done.

7 Cool on wire rack. Frost with Confectioners' Icing. Decorate with almonds and red and green cherries.

Panettone (pahn-uh-TOE-nay)

A tremendous favorite in Italy throughout the year but especially at Christmas, panettone (meaning "little loaf") is a delight anywhere. Yields 1 loaf.

Ingredients

2–3 cups	flour
1 tablespoon	active dry yeast
¼ cup	milk
¼ cup	honey
4 tablespoons	unsalted butter
½ teaspoon	salt
1 teaspoon	crushed aniseeds
2	eggs
¼ cup	golden raisins
¼ cup	currants
¼ cup	chopped candied citron
Glaze	
1	egg, beaten with 1 tablespoon water

Preparation

1 Combine 1½ cups flour and yeast in mixing bowl. Heat milk, honey, butter, salt, and aniseeds to hot (120°–130°F). Mix thoroughly.

2 Add milk mixture and eggs to dry ingredients. Mix thoroughly.

3 Stir in raisins, currants, citron, and enough remaining flour to make a soft dough.

4 Knead on lightly floured surface until smooth—about 10 minutes. Place in greased bowl, turning to coat top. Cover; let rise in warm place until double—about 1½ hours.

5 Punch down dough. Cover; let set for 10 minutes.

6 Four different ways of shaping:
(a) Shape into 1 ball; place on greased baking sheet.
(b) Place in a well-greased charlotte mold or similar baking pan. Brush top with melted butter.
(c) Shape into 1 ball. Place in greased, deep, 7-inch round cake pan.
(d) Shape into ball and place in a well-greased (especially grooves) coffee can.

7 Cover; let rise until double—about 30 minutes. Cut a cross on top of dough. Make glaze and brush on loaf.

8 Bake in a preheated 350°F oven 35–45 minutes or until done. Cool on wire rack.

Pandoro di Verona (pon-DOH-ro dee Vair-OH-na)
Golden Bread of Verona

This delicate bread is a favorite—especially at Christmas—in Verona, the home of Romeo and Juliet. Yields 1 loaf.

Ingredients

1 tablespoon	active dry yeast	
¼ cup	warm water (105°–115°F)	
2–2½ cups	flour	
⅓ cup	sugar	
2 tablespoons	unsalted butter, melted	
½ teaspoon	salt	
1	egg	
3	egg yolks	
1 teaspoon	grated lemon or orange peel	
½ teaspoon	vanilla extract	
1 stick	cold unsalted butter, cut in thin slices	
	sugar	
	vanilla confectioners' sugar (p. 215)	

Preparation

1 Dissolve yeast in warm water. Set aside for 5 minutes. Combine 1½ cups flour, sugar, melted butter, salt, egg, egg yolks, lemon or orange peel, vanilla, and yeast mixture in mixing bowl. Mix thoroughly.

2 Add enough remaining flour to make a soft dough. Knead on a lightly floured surface until smooth—about 10 minutes.

3 Place in greased bowl, turning to coat top. Cover; let rise until double—about 1 hour.

4 Roll into a 9 x 18-inch rectangle. Place half cold butter on center third. Fold left third over top of center third. Place other half cold butter on top. Fold right third over top.

5 Roll into a rectangle; fold in thirds as before. Chill for 1 hour. Repeat 2 more times.

6 Grease 2-inch-deep, 8-inch round pan. Shape to fit pan. Butter top of loaf and sprinkle lightly with sugar. Cover; let rise in warm place until double—about 45 minutes.

7 Bake in a preheated 400°F oven 15 minutes; then lower heat to 350°F and bake 35–45 minutes or until cake tester comes out clean. Cool on wire rack. Sprinkle with vanilla confectioners' sugar.

Pangiallo (pahn-JAHL-lo)

Romans love this Christmas bread, with its bounty of spices, nuts, and candied fruit. Pangiallo is so deliciously heavy with fruit and nuts that it won't rise very much. Yields 1 loaf.

Ingredients

½ tablespoon	active dry yeast
¼ cup	warm water (105°–115°F)
2 tablespoons	unsalted butter
¼ cup	sugar
1 cup	flour
¼ teaspoon	ground cinnamon
¼ teaspoon	ground cloves
¼ teaspoon	grated nutmeg
¼ teaspoon	ground allspice
½ cup	chopped almonds
½ cup	chopped filberts
½ cup	chopped mixed candied fruit
½ cup	pignolia nuts
1 teaspoon	grated lemon peel
	confectioners' sugar

Preparation

1 Dissolve yeast in 2 tablespoons warm water. Set aside for 5 minutes. Heat 2 tablespoons warm water, butter, and sugar in saucepan until sugar is dissolved. Cool to warm.

2 Combine flour, yeast mixture, water mixture, cinnamon, cloves, nutmeg, and allspice in mixing bowl. Mix thoroughly.

3 Add almonds, filberts, candied fruit, pignolia nuts, and lemon peel. Mix thoroughly.

4 Place in greased bowl, turning to coat top. Cover; put in warm place for 3 hours.

5 Knead on lightly floured surface about 5 minutes. Shape into ball. Place on greased baking sheet. Cover with plastic wrap and towel. Place in refrigerator overnight.

Topping

1 tablespoon water
2 tablespoons sugar
¼ teaspoon ground cinnamon
1 tablespoon vegetable oil
3 tablespoons flour

6 Heat water and sugar until sugar dissolves. Add cinnamon, vegetable oil, and flour to water mixture. Remove dough from refrigerator. Brush topping on loaf while heating oven.

7 Bake in a preheated 375°F oven about 45–55 minutes or until done. Cool on wire rack. Sprinkle with confectioners' sugar before serving.

Spanish Christmas Loaf

*This bread makes a haunting addition to Christmas in Spain,
and you too will love its almond fragrance. Yields 1 loaf.*

Ingredients

½ tablespoon	active dry yeast
⅓ cup	warm milk (105°–115°F)
2–3 cups	flour
½ teaspoon	salt
2 tablespoons	sugar
1	egg
¼ teaspoon	almond extract
¼ cup	ground almonds
Filling	
1 tablespoon	unsalted butter, melted
½ cup	mixed chopped candied fruit
1	egg
2 tablespoons	sugar
¼ cup	ground almonds

Preparation

1 Dissolve yeast in warm milk. Set aside for 5 minutes. Combine 1½ cups flour, salt, sugar, yeast mixture, and egg in mixing bowl. Mix thoroughly.

2 Add almond extract and ground almonds and enough remaining flour to make a soft dough. Knead on lightly floured surface until smooth—about 10 minutes.

3 Place in greased bowl, turning to coat top. Cover; let rise in warm place until double—about 1 hour.

4 Punch down dough. Make into rectangle. Brush with melted butter, and sprinkle with candied fruit. Combine egg, sugar, and ground almonds. Spread over fruit. Roll up jelly-roll style. Pinch seam and ends to seal. Place seam side down on greased baking sheet.

5 Cover; let rise in warm place until double—about 30 minutes. Bake in a preheated 350°F oven 30 minutes or until done. Cool on wire rack.

English Christmas Bread

Plum pudding has a rival in this rich, fruit and nut filled bread for a treat that will enhance your Christmas dinner. Yields 1 loaf.

Ingredients

3–4 cups	flour
½ tablespoon	active dry yeast
⅓ cup	water
½ tablespoon	ground allspice
½ teaspoon	caraway seeds
¼ teaspoon	grated nutmeg
3 tablespoons	unsalted butter
½ teaspoon	salt
3 tablespoons	sugar
1	egg
3 tablespoons	chopped mixed candied fruit
3 tablespoons	golden raisins
3 tablespoons	slivered almonds
	Confectioners' Icing (p. 208)
	whole almonds
	candied cherries

Preparation

1 Combine 2 cups flour and yeast in a mixing bowl. Heat water, allspice, caraway seeds, nutmeg, butter, salt, and sugar to hot (120°–130°F).

2 Add water mixture to flour and yeast. Mix thoroughly. Add egg, mixed fruit, raisins, and slivered almonds.

3 Add enough remaining flour to make a soft dough. Knead on lightly floured surface until smooth—about 10 minutes.

4 Place in greased bowl, turning to coat top. Cover; let rise in warm place until double—about 1 hour.

5 Punch down dough. Shape into round loaf. Place on greased baking sheet.

6 Cover; let rise in warm place until double—about 45 minutes. Bake in a preheated 350°F oven about 45–55 minutes or until done.

7 Cool on wire rack. Frost with Confectioners' Icing. Decorate with almonds and candied cherries.

Wiggs

The English name Wiggs for this bread originally meant "wedges," since the round loaf is scored to permit division into eight spicy wedges. Yields 1 loaf.

Ingredients

1 tablespoon	active dry yeast
2 tablespoons	warm water (105°–115°F)
¼ cup	sugar
½ teaspoon	salt
4 tablespoons	unsalted butter
⅓ cup	milk
2½–3 cups	flour
¼ teaspoon	ground ginger
¼ teaspoon	grated nutmeg
¼ teaspoon	ground mace
¼ teaspoon	ground cloves
1 tablespoon	caraway seeds, lightly crushed
1	egg
2 tablespoons	currants

Preparation

1 Dissolve yeast in warm water. Set aside for 5 minutes. Heat sugar, salt, butter, and milk to warm (105°–115°F).

2 Combine 2 cups flour, ginger, nutmeg, mace, cloves, and caraway seeds in mixing bowl. Add yeast mixture and milk mixture. Mix thoroughly.

3 Add egg, currants, and enough remaining flour to make a soft dough.

4 Knead on lightly floured surface until smooth—about 10 minutes. Place in greased bowl, turning to coat top.

5 Cover; let rise in warm place until double—about 1½ hours. Punch down dough. Shape into a round loaf. Place in greased 2-inch-deep, 8-inch round pan.

6 Cover; let rise in warm place until double—about 30–45 minutes. Using scissors or sharp knife, make 4 deep cuts across top of loaf, to permit division into 8 wedges (wiggs). (See illustration.)

7 Bake in a preheated 350°F oven about 45–55 minutes or until done. Cool on wire rack.

154

Boxing Day Cake

In Britain, Boxing Day is the first weekday after Christmas, a legal holiday on which gifts (often boxed) are given to mail carriers and others in similar occupations. You'll find the spicy bread here perfect for an after-Christmas treat. Yields 1 loaf.

Ingredients

½ tablespoon	active dry yeast
2 tablespoons	warm water (105°–115°F)
½ cup	milk
2 tablespoons	sugar
2 tablespoons	unsalted butter
½ teaspoon	salt
2–2½ cups	flour
½ teaspoon	grated lemon peel
1 teaspoon	ground cinnamon
¼ teaspoon	ground allspice
¼ teaspoon	grated nutmeg
¼ teaspoon	ground cloves
¼ cup	light brown sugar, firmly packed
1	egg
½ cup	currants
½ cup	dark raisins
⅓ cup	chopped mixed candied fruit

Preparation

1 Dissolve yeast in warm water. Set aside for 5 minutes. Heat milk, sugar, butter, and salt to warm (105°–115°F).

2 Combine 1 cup flour, lemon peel, cinnamon, allspice, nutmeg, cloves, and brown sugar in mixing bowl. Add yeast mixture and milk mixture. Mix thoroughly.

3 Add egg, currants, raisins, candied fruit, and enough remaining flour to make a soft dough.

4 Knead on lightly floured surface until smooth—about 10 minutes. Place in greased bowl, turning to coat top.

5 Cover; let rise in warm place until double—about 1 hour.

6 Punch down dough. Shape into a round loaf. Place in greased 2-inch-deep, 8-inch round pan.

7 Cover; let rise in warm place until double—about 30–45 minutes.

8 Bake in a preheated 350°F oven about 1 hour or until done. Five minutes before baking is completed, brush with additional milk and sprinkle lightly with more sugar. Cool on wire rack.

155

Yankee Christmas Bread

Potatoes—yes, potatoes—are a feature of this rich Christmas bread. An old-time favorite in New England farmhouses. Yields 1 loaf.

Ingredients

1 small	potato, peeled and sliced
⅔ cup	warm unsalted potato water (105°–115°F)
1 tablespoon	active dry yeast
⅔ cup	milk
3½–4 cups	flour
6 tablespoons	unsalted butter
½ cup	sugar
1	egg
½ teaspoon	salt
1 cup	golden raisins
⅓ cup	chopped candied citron
⅓ cup	chopped candied orange peel
2 tablespoons	unsalted butter, melted
2 teaspoons	sugar
1 teaspoon	ground cinnamon

Preparation

1 Boil potato in unsalted water until very tender. Drain, and set aside ⅔ cup of the water. Cool potato to warm. Mash.

2 Dissolve yeast in warm unsalted potato water. Set aside for 5 minutes. Heat milk to warm (105°–115°F) and add to yeast mixture.

3 Stir in mashed potato and 1½ cups flour. Mix thoroughly. Cover; let rise in warm place about 1 hour.

4 Cream butter with sugar; mix thoroughly. Add egg and salt.

5 Add this mixture to the yeast and potato mixture. Add enough remaining flour to make a soft dough. Mix thoroughly.

6 Knead in the raisins, citron, and orange peel.

7 Knead on lightly floured surface until smooth—about 10 minutes.

8 Cover; let rise until double—about 45 minutes. Punch down dough. Shape into round loaf.

9 Place in greased 2-inch-deep, 8-inch round cake pan. Brush top of loaf with melted butter and sugar and cinnamon mixture.

10 Cover; let rise in warm place until double—about 1 hour. Bake in a preheated 350°F oven about 1 hour or until done. Cool on wire rack.

Poppy Seed Loaf

A scrumptious poppy seed and honey filling makes this bread a Canadian favorite, especially at Christmastime. For poppy seed fanatics—and all others! Yields 1 loaf.

Hungarian - Kovanek.

Ingredients

½ tablespoon	active dry yeast
1 tablespoon	warm water (105°–115°F)
1–2 cups	flour
½ teaspoon	salt
⅓ cup	sugar
1 teaspoon	grated orange peel
2 tablespoons	unsalted butter, softened
¼ cup	warm milk (105°–115°F)
1	egg, separated
1	egg yolk, beaten with 1 tablespoon water

Filling

2 tablespoons	unsalted butter
1 tablespoon	honey
1 tablespoon	cream
⅓ cup	poppy seeds
2 tablespoons	chopped candied orange peel
¼ cup	chopped almonds

Preparation

1 Dissolve yeast in warm water. Set aside for 5 minutes. Combine 1½ cups flour, salt, sugar, and orange peel in mixing bowl. Mix thoroughly.

2 Stir in yeast mixture, butter, warm milk, and egg yolk. Mix thoroughly.

3 Add enough remaining flour to make a soft dough. Knead on lightly floured surface until smooth—about 10 minutes.

4 Place in greased bowl, turning to coat top. Cover; let rise in warm place until double—about 1 hour.

5 Prepare the poppy seed filling: cream butter and honey together in small mixing bowl. Add the cream, poppy seeds, orange peel, and almonds. Mix thoroughly.

6 Punch down dough. Roll the dough into a rectangle 6 x 12 inches. Beat egg white until it forms stiff peaks. Fold egg white into poppy seed mixture.

7 Spread the poppy seed mixture evenly on the dough, leaving a 1-inch border all around. Roll up the dough jelly-roll style; pinch sides and ends to seal. Place on greased baking sheet.

8 Cover; let rise in a warm place 30 minutes or until double. Brush egg-yolk mixture on loaf. Bake in a preheated 350°F oven 30–40 minutes or until done. Cool on wire rack.

Christmas Coffee Can Loaf

Bake this colorful loaf in a coffee can for a bread that is as distinctive in shape as it is in taste. This bread makes an excellent gift, which I have sometimes sent to my children's teachers. Yields 3 cakes.

Ingredients

3–4 cups	flour
¼ cup	sugar
1 teaspoon	salt
1 tablespoon	active dry yeast
1 cup	milk
4 tablespoons	unsalted butter
1	egg
½ teaspoon	almond extract
¾ cup	chopped mixed candied fruit
¼ cup	golden raisins
¼ cup	chopped almonds
	Confectioners' Icing (p. 208), if desired

Preparation

1 Combine 2 cups flour, sugar, salt, and yeast in mixing bowl. Heat milk and butter to hot (120°–130°F). Add egg, almond extract, and milk mixture to flour mixture. Mix thoroughly.

2 Stir in candied fruit, raisins, and almonds.

3 Add enough remaining flour to make a soft dough. Knead on lightly floured surface until smooth—about 10 minutes.

4 Place in greased bowl, turning to coat top. Cover; let rise in warm place until double—about 1 hour. Punch down dough.

5 Divide into 3 pieces and place in 3 well-greased 1-pound coffee cans. (Be sure, however, that each coffee can is no more than half full.) *Be sure to grease the grooves well.*

6 Cover; let rise in warm place until double—about 1 hour.

7 Bake in a preheated 350°F oven 45–55 minutes or until done. Cool on wire rack.

8 If desired, frost tops with Confectioners' Icing.

Candy Cane Coffee Cake I

Here are two irresistible but distinct candy cane cakes. The first is the simpler; the second is two-toned with two different fillings. Each recipe yields 1 cake.

Ingredients

½ cup	dairy sour cream
½ tablespoon	active dry yeast
2 tablespoons	warm water (105°–115°F)
1½–2 cups	flour
1 tablespoon	unsalted butter, softened
1 tablespoon	sugar
½ teaspoon	salt
1	egg
½ cup	finely chopped dried apricots
½ cup	finely chopped maraschino cherries
	Thin Confectioners' Icing (p. 208)

Preparation

1 Heat sour cream to warm (105°–115°F) over low heat. Dissolve yeast in warm water. Set aside for 5 minutes.

2 Combine 1 cup flour, sour cream, butter, sugar, salt, and egg in mixing bowl. Add yeast mixture. Mix thoroughly. Add enough remaining flour to make a soft dough.

3 Knead dough on lightly floured surface until smooth—about 10 minutes.

4 Place in greased bowl, turning to coat top. Cover; let rise in warm place until double—about 1 hour.

5 Punch down dough. Roll into a rectangle 6 x 12 inches. Mix apricots and cherries. (If you don't like this filling, try another one from Chapter 20.) Spread mixture down center third of rectangle. Using scissors, snip 2-inch cuts every ½ inch on long sides of rectangle. Crisscross strips on top of filling. Place on greased sheet.

6 Stretch dough until 18 inches long. Curve one end to form cane handle.

7 Bake in a preheated 375°F oven 15–20 minutes or until done.

8 Make thin Confectioners' Icing. Drizzle icing over cane while still warm. Decorate with cherry halves.

• **Note:** You can make a wreath instead of a candy cane by forming a circle and pinching ends together. Ice as the candy cane.

159

Candy Cane Coffee Cake II

Ingredients

2–3 cups	flour
¼ cup	sugar
½ teaspoon	salt
1 tablespoon	active dry yeast
½ cup	milk
4 tablespoons	unsalted butter
2 tablespoons	water
2	eggs
	red food coloring

Red Filling

3 tablespoons	chopped candied red cherries
2 tablespoons	chopped candied pineapple
1 tablespoon	chopped golden raisins
1 tablespoon	unsalted butter, softened

Preparation

1 Combine 1 cup flour, sugar, salt, and yeast in a bowl. Heat milk, butter, and water in saucepan to hot (120°–130°F).

2 Add milk mixture to dry ingredients. Mix thoroughly. Add eggs and enough remaining flour to make a soft dough. Knead on lightly floured surface until smooth—about 10 minutes.

3 Divide dough in half. Add a few drops of red coloring to one of the halves.

4 Grease 2 bowls and place dough in bowls, turning to coat tops. Cover; let rise in warm place until double—about 1 hour.

5 Make red filling by mixing red cherries, pineapple, raisins, and butter together. Make white filling by mixing almonds, coconut, and butter together.

6 Punch down dough in each bowl. Roll out into 9 x 12-inch rectangles (one red and one white).

7 Spread red filling on red dough, leaving 1-inch border; roll up jelly-roll style. Do the same to the other filling and dough. Place side by side on a greased baking sheet.

White Filling

3 tablespoons   chopped almonds

3 tablespoons   shredded coconut

1 tablespoon   unsalted butter, softened

Glaze

1   egg, beaten with 1 tablespoon
                 water

Frosting

1 cup   confectioners' sugar

2 tablespoons   unsalted butter

¼ teaspoon   almond extract

3 tablespoons   milk

pinch   salt

                 red food coloring (for red
                 frosting only)

8   Twist together and shape into a cane. Let rise in warm place until double—about 30 minutes. Make glaze and brush on loaf.

9   Bake in a preheated 350°F oven 20–25 minutes or until done. Cool on wire rack.

10 Make frosting. Divide in half and add red food coloring to one half. Frost white dough with white frosting and red dough with red frosting.

Evergreen Coffee Cake

Looking like a snow-covered fir tree, this filled coffee cake will add to the festive air of your holiday table. Yields 1 cake.

Ingredients

1 tablespoon	active dry yeast
¼ cup	warm water (105°–115°F)
½ cup	milk
½ teaspoon	salt
3 tablespoons	sugar
½ teaspoon	grated lemon peel
4 tablespoons	unsalted butter
2½–3 cups	flour
1	egg
	candied green and red cherries

Filling

¼ cup	chopped walnuts
3 tablespoons	light brown sugar
2 teaspoons	ground cinnamon
1 teaspoon	grated lemon peel
2 tablespoons	dark raisins, if desired
	melted butter

Preparation

1 Dissolve yeast in warm water. Set aside for 5 minutes. Heat milk, salt, sugar, lemon peel, and butter to warm (105°–115°F).

2 Combine 1½ cups flour, milk mixture, yeast mixture, and egg. Mix thoroughly.

3 Add enough remaining flour to make a soft dough. Knead on lightly floured surface until smooth—about 10 minutes.

4 Place in greased bowl, turning to coat top. Cover. Let rise in warm place until double—about 1 hour.

5 Combine walnuts, brown sugar, cinnamon, lemon peel, and raisins in a small bowl.

6 Punch down dough. Make dough into a triangle 15 inches on each side. Brush with melted butter. Sprinkle on filling.

7 Roll dough along the base, starting at each of the 2 lower corners, until rolled halves meet at center. Pinch seam; turn dough over. Place on greased baking sheet; flatten slightly. Using scissors, cut intervals to within 1 inch of center down each side. Turn cut sections up for the branches. Cut off the bottom branch from each side. Place together at the bottom, forming the base of the tree.

8 Cover; place in warm place until double—about 30 minutes.

9 Bake in a preheated 350°F oven about 25–35 minutes or until done. Cool on wire rack.

Icing

1 cup   confectioners' sugar

2–4 tablespoons   milk

½ teaspoon   vanilla extract

10   Make icing; frost loaf. Decorate with candied cherries.

Christmas Tree Bubble Coffee Cake I

Here's a coffee cake that looks beautiful, is fun to eat (you pull it apart), and tastes like a dream! The first recipe features a pineapple flavor, the second cardamom. Each recipe yields 1 cake.

Ingredients

1½ ounces	cream cheese
3 tablespoons	milk
2 tablespoons	sugar
1 tablespoon	unsalted butter
¼ teaspoon	salt
1 teaspoon	active dry yeast
1–1½ cups	flour
1	egg
½ cup	drained, crushed pineapple
	reserved pineapple syrup
	Confectioners' Icing (p. 208)
	green food coloring
	red and green maraschino cherries

Preparation

1 Combine cream cheese, milk, sugar, butter, and salt in saucepan. Heat until cheese and butter are melted (120°–130°F).

2 In large bowl, combine yeast, 1 cup flour, and cream cheese mixture. Add egg. Mix thoroughly.

3 Add drained pineapple and enough remaining flour to make a soft dough. Knead on lightly floured surface until smooth—about 10 minutes.

4 Place in greased bowl, turning to coat top. Cover; let rise in warm place until double—about 1 hour.

5 Punch down dough. Knead about 3 minutes. Divide dough into 25 equal pieces and make balls. Arrange in triangle, using 2 pairs of balls for trunk. (See drawing.) Place on greased baking sheet.

6 Cover; let rise until double—about 30 minutes. Bake in a preheated 350°F oven about 30 minutes or until done.

7 Mix icing using reserved pineapple syrup. Drizzle over warm bread. Decorate with red and green cherries.

Julbrod, page 125 ▶
Polish Christmas Bread, page 140 ▶

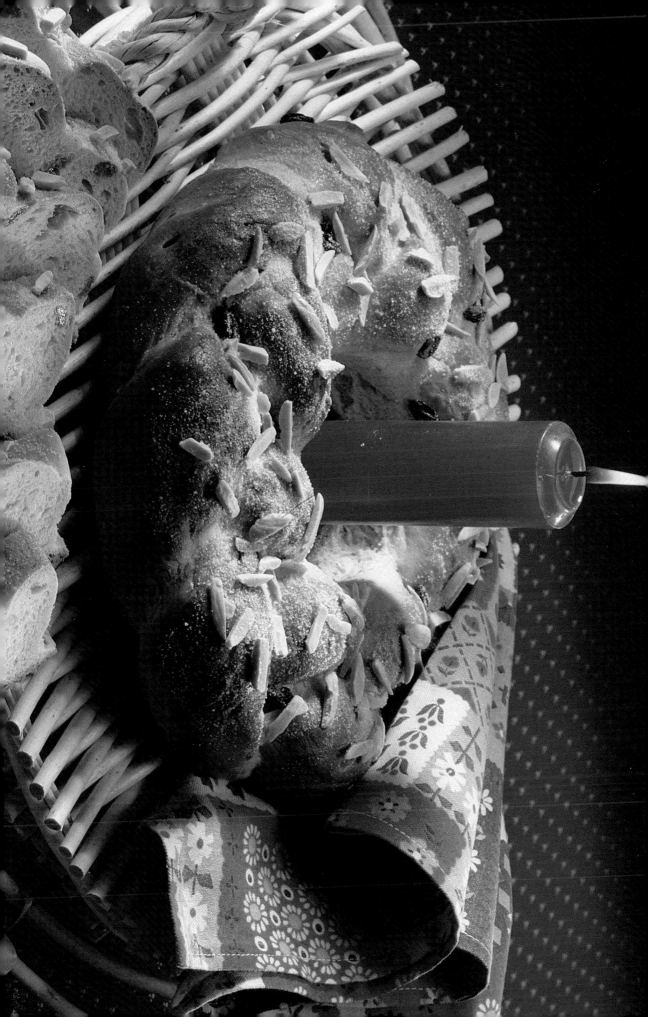

Christmas Tree Bubble Coffee Cake II

Ingredients

½ tablespoon	active dry yeast	
2 tablespoons	warm water (105°–115°F)	
⅓ cup	milk	
2 tablespoons	sugar	
½ teaspoon	salt	
3 tablespoons	unsalted butter, softened	
½ teaspoon	ground cardamom	
1½–2½ cups	flour	
1	egg	
	Confectioners' Icing (p. 208), if desired	
	candied cherries	

Preparation

1 Dissolve yeast in warm water. Set aside for 5 minutes. Heat milk, sugar, salt, butter, and cardamom to warm (105°–115°F).

2 Combine 1 cup flour, milk mixture, and yeast mixture in mixing bowl. Mix thoroughly.

3 Add egg and enough remaining flour to make a soft dough. Knead on lightly floured surface until smooth—about 10 minutes.

4 Place in greased bowl, turning to coat top. Cover; let rise in warm place until double—about 1 hour.

5 Punch down dough. Divide dough into 17 equal pieces and make balls. Form Christmas tree as in previous recipe on greased baking sheet.

6 Cover; let rise in warm place until double—about 30 minutes.

7 Bake in a preheated 350°F oven 20–25 minutes or until done. Cool on wire rack.

8 If desired, drizzle with Confectioners' Icing. Decorate with candied cherries.

Lemon Candy Canes

These individual lemony candy canes make a unique and very popular Christmas treat. Excellent for a snack at any time during the holidays. Yields 12 canes.

Ingredients

½ tablespoon	active dry yeast
¼ cup	warm water (105°–115°F)
1½ –2½ cups	flour
1 tablespoon	sugar
½ teaspoon	salt
½ tablespoon	grated lemon peel
1	egg
¼ cup	warm dairy sour cream (105°–115°F)
2 tablespoons	unsalted butter, softened
	chopped candied lemon peel

Filling

¼ cup	chopped walnuts
¼ cup	sugar
2 tablespoons	unsalted butter

Preparation

1 Dissolve yeast in warm water. Set aside for 5 minutes. Combine 1 cup flour, sugar, salt, and grated lemon peel in mixing bowl. Add yeast mixture, egg, warm sour cream, and butter. Mix thoroughly.

2 Add enough remaining flour to make a soft dough.

3 Knead on lightly floured surface until smooth—about 10 minutes. Place in greased bowl, turning to coat top.

4 Cover; let rise in warm place until smooth—about 1 hour.

5 Punch down dough. Roll dough to an 8 x 12-inch rectangle. Make filling.

6 Spread with half the filling. Fold in half lengthwise. Pinch together long edges. Cut across in 1-inch strips. Twist strips.

7 Place on greased baking sheet. Form canes. Cover; let rise in warm place until double—about 30 minutes.

8 Bake in a preheated 375°F oven 12–15 minutes or until done.

Icing

½ cup	confectioners' sugar
2 teaspoons	lemon juice
2 teaspoons	water
¼ teaspoon	vanilla extract

9 Make icing and frost canes. Decorate with candied lemon peel.

Candy Cane Twists

These pencil-thin delicacies are a charming addition to any Christmas cocktail party. Watch how fast they go!
Yields 24 canes.

Ingredients

1 tablespoon	active dry yeast
⅓ cup	warm water (105°–115°F)
3–4 cups	flour
½ cup	warm milk (105°–115°F)
⅓ cup	sugar
½ teaspoon	salt
4 tablespoons	unsalted butter
1	egg
1 cup	quartered red candied cherries
	unsalted butter, melted
	Confectioners' Icing (p. 208), if desired
	red food coloring

Preparation

1 Dissolve yeast in warm water. Set aside for 5 minutes.

2 Combine 2 cups flour, warm milk, sugar, salt, butter, egg, and yeast mixture in mixing bowl. Mix thoroughly.

3 Add enough remaining flour to make a soft dough. Knead on lightly floured surface until smooth—about 10 minutes.

4 Place in greased bowl, turning to coat top. Cover; let rise in a warm place until double—about 1 hour.

5 Punch down dough. Knead in cherries. Let rise a second time until double—about 30 minutes.

6 Divide in half. Roll each into a 7 x 12-inch rectangle. Working on the long side, cut twelve 1-inch strips (this makes 12 canes).

7 Twist. Place 1 inch apart on greased baking sheet. Shape into canes. Press ends of canes firmly down.

8 Brush with melted butter. Cover; let rise until double—about 20 minutes.

9 Bake in a preheated 375°F oven about 12 minutes or until done.

10 If desired, make Confectioners' Icing. Divide in half; place in 2 separate bowls. Put red food coloring in one bowl; mix thoroughly. Frost with Confectioners' Icing while warm. With red icing, make stripes after white has set.

Holiday Bubble Wreath

*This wreath is meant to be pulled apart by the people eating it.
You'll find it an excellent icebreaker at any gathering. Yields 1 cake.*

Ingredients

½ cup	milk	
2 tablespoons	sugar	
2 tablespoons	unsalted butter	
¼ teaspoon	salt	
½ tablespoon	active dry yeast	
2 tablespoons	warm water (105°–115°F)	
1–2 cups	flour	
1	egg	

Topping

3 tablespoons	unsalted butter	
1 tablespoon	light corn syrup	
⅓ cup	light brown sugar, firmly packed	
	pecan halves	
1 teaspoon	ground cinnamon	

Preparation

1 Heat milk, sugar, butter, and salt to warm (105°–115°F). Dissolve yeast in warm water. Set aside for 5 minutes.

2 Combine 1 cup flour, milk mixture, yeast mixture, and egg. Mix thoroughly.

3 Add enough remaining flour to make a soft dough. Knead on lightly floured surface until smooth—about 10 minutes.

4 Place in greased bowl, turning to coat top. Cover; let rise in warm place until double—about 1 hour. Punch down dough.

5 Melt 1 tablespoon butter; add corn syrup and brown sugar. Pour into greased 6-cup Bundt pan. Place pecan halves on this mixture in a decorative pattern.

6 Cut 32 equal pieces, and shape dough into 32 small balls. Melt 2 tablespoons butter; add brown sugar and cinnamon. Roll each ball in this mixture.

7 Place 16 balls in bottom of Bundt pan. Then place another layer of 16 balls over the spaces among balls in the first layer. Cover; let rise in warm place for 30 minutes.

8 Place a baking sheet under lower rack while baking so dough won't fall on oven floor. Bake in a preheated 375°F oven 40 minutes or until done. Cool in pan for 20 minutes. Cool on wire rack.

Cherry Christmas Wreath

With a cream cheese and cherry filling, this wreath goes beautifully with coffee when friends drop in. Yields 1 cake.

Ingredients

½ tablespoon	active dry yeast
¼ cup	warm water (105°–115°F)
¼ teaspoon	salt
¼ cup	sugar
4 tablespoons	unsalted butter
¼ cup	milk
2½–3 cups	flour
1	egg
	Confectioners' Icing (p. 208)
	green and red candied cherries

Filling

3 ounces	cream cheese
½ cup	cherry pie filling
⅓ cup	finely chopped almonds
1 teaspoon	grated orange peel

Preparation

1 Dissolve yeast in warm water. Set aside for 5 minutes. Heat salt, sugar, butter, and milk to warm (105°–115°F).

2 Combine 1½ cups flour, yeast mixture, and milk mixture in mixing bowl. Mix thoroughly.

3 Add egg and enough remaining flour to make a soft dough.

4 Knead on lightly floured surface until smooth—about 10 minutes. Place in greased bowl, turning to coat top.

5 Cover; let rise in warm place until double—about 1 hour. Combine ingredients for filling. Mix thoroughly.

6 Punch down dough. Roll into a 9 x 18-inch rectangle. Spread filling down center third. Roll up jelly-roll style, and pinch seam. Form into a circle, and pinch ends. Place on greased baking sheet.

7 With scissors, cut 1-inch intervals. Turn cut sections up.

8 Bake in a preheated 350°F oven 30 minutes or until done. Cool on wire rack. Make icing. Drizzle on loaf, and decorate with cherries.

Angel Faces

Here is Christmas fun for children and good eating for everyone—angel faces that are as enjoyable to make as they are to eat. Yields 18 faces.

Ingredients

½ tablespoon	active dry yeast	
2 tablespoons	warm water (105°–115°F)	
2 tablespoons	sugar	
⅓ cup	milk	
2 tablespoons	unsalted butter	
¼ teaspoon	salt	
2–2½ cups	flour	
1 teaspoon	crushed aniseeds	
½ tablespoon	grated lemon peel	
1	egg	
	dark raisins or currants	

Glaze

1	egg yolk, beaten with 1 tablespoon milk	

Preparation

1 Dissolve yeast in warm water. Set aside for 5 minutes.

2 Heat sugar, milk, butter, and salt to warm (105°–115°F). Combine 1 cup flour, aniseeds, lemon peel, milk mixture, and yeast mixture in mixing bowl. Mix thoroughly.

3 Add egg and enough remaining flour to make a soft dough. Knead on lightly floured surface until smooth—about 10 minutes.

4 Place in greased bowl, turning to coat top. Cover; let rise in warm place until double—about 1 hour.

5 Punch down dough. Divide dough into 18 pieces. Make faces 2 inches in diameter; use excess dough for hair, hat, etc. Moisten with water to attach faces. Use raisins or currants for features.

6 Place on greased baking sheet. Cover; let rise in warm place about 15–20 minutes. *Do not let rise too long—dough will lose its shape when baking.*

7 Brush with water. Bake in a preheated 350°F oven 20–30 minutes or until done. Brush with water twice during baking. Make glaze and brush on faces 5 minutes before end of baking. Cool on wire rack.

• **Note:** Try your own ideas, including whole dolls. (Make arms and legs pencil thin.)

Santa Claus Face

This bread, in the form of Santa Claus's face, always adds to the Christmas delight of children. Yields 1 face.

Ingredients

½ tablespoon	active dry yeast
2 tablespoons	warm water (105°–115°F)
⅓ cup	milk
3 tablespoons	unsalted butter
1 tablespoon	sugar
¼ teaspoon	salt
½ teaspoon	ground cardamom
2–2½ cups	flour
1	egg
	Confectioners' Icing (p. 208), if desired
	red food coloring
	shredded coconut, if desired

Glaze

1	egg, beaten with 1 tablespoon water

Preparation

1 Dissolve yeast in warm water. Set aside for 5 minutes. Heat milk, butter, sugar, salt, and cardamom to warm (105°–115°F).

2 Combine 1½ cups flour, yeast mixture, milk mixture, and egg in mixing bowl. Mix thoroughly.

3 Add enough remaining flour to make a soft dough. Knead on lightly floured surface until smooth—about 10 minutes.

4 Place in greased bowl, turning to coat top. Cover; let rise in warm place until double—about 1 hour.

5 Punch down dough. Take about ⅔ of dough; from 1 piece make a round face. With a second piece, shape Santa's hat tipped to one side. Place on greased baking sheet. Using the remaining third, make: a mouth—½-inch ball; a nose—1-inch ball; the cheeks—two 1-inch balls, slightly flattened; a pompom—2-inch ball; the eyebrows—two ¾-inch ropes; a mustache—two 1½-inch oval shapes, slightly flattened; the trim for the hat—two 6-inch long ropes, twisted together and placed above eyebrows; and a beard—with remaining dough make a triangle shape under mouth. (See drawing, page 173.) Make glaze and brush on loaf.

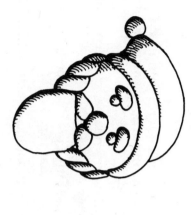

6 Cover; let rise in a warm place about 15 minutes. Do not let rise too long—dough will lose its shape when baking. Bake in a preheated 350°F oven about 30 minutes or until done. Cool on wire rack.

7 If desired, make Confectioners' Icing. Use 1 drop of red coloring to make face pink. Use a little more red for deeper pink on mouth, nose, and cheeks. Use enough coloring to produce bright red for hat. For the rest (pompom, beard, mustache, eyebrows, and hat trim), frost with white. Use coconut if desired.

Frosted Christmas Treats

You can make this frosted, fruit-filled bread in a variety of sizes and shapes—from miniatures to round or standard loaf.

Ingredients

1 tablespoon	active dry yeast
2 tablespoons	warm water (105°–115°F)
2–3 cups	flour
½ cup	warm milk (105°–115°F)
¼ cup	sugar
¼ teaspoon	grated nutmeg
½ teaspoon	ground allspice
2 tablespoons	unsalted butter
½ teaspoon	salt
1	egg
⅓ cup	golden raisins
⅓ cup	chopped mixed candied fruit
	Confectioners' Icing (p. 208), if desired
	walnut halves or candied cherries

Preparation

1 Dissolve yeast in warm water. Set aside for 5 minutes. Combine 1½ cups flour, warm milk, sugar, nutmeg, allspice, butter, and salt in mixing bowl. Mix thoroughly.

2 Add yeast mixture and egg. Mix. Add raisins, candied fruit, and enough remaining flour to make a soft dough.

3 Knead on lightly floured surface until smooth—about 10 minutes. Place in greased bowl, turning to coat top.

4 Cover; let rise in warm place until double—about 1 hour. Punch down dough.

5 Make in any of the following shapes:

Standard Loaf

6 Shape dough into loaf. Place in greased 4½ x 8½-inch pan.

7 Cover; let rise in warm place until double—about 45–60 minutes. Bake in a preheated 350°F oven 45–60 minutes or until done. Cool on wire rack.

8 If desired, drizzle top of loaf with Confectioners' Icing. Trim with walnut halves or candied cherries.

Round Loaf

6 Shape dough into a ball. Place ball on greased baking sheet, flattening slightly.

7 Cover; let rise in warm place until double—about 1 hour.

8 Bake in preheated 350°F oven about 30—40 minutes or until done. Cool on wire rack.

9 If desired, drizzle top with Confectioners' Icing. Trim with walnut halves or candied cherries.

Individual Loaves

6 Divide dough into 4 equal pieces. Shape each piece into a loaf and place in greased 3 x 5½-inch loaf pans.

7 Cover; let rise in warm place until double—about 30 minutes. Bake in preheated 350°F oven 20—30 minutes or until done. Cool on wire rack.

8 If desired, drizzle top of each with Confectioners' Icing. Trim with walnut halves or candied cherries.

Miniature Treats

6 Shape dough into 12 balls. Place in greased muffin pan. Cover; let rise in warm place until double—about 20 minutes.

7 Bake in preheated 350°F oven about 20—25 minutes or until done. Cool on wire rack.

8 If desired, drizzle the top of each with Confectioners' Icing. Trim with walnut halves or candied cherries.

Sourdough Yule Bread

A sourdough treat filled with nuts and colorful fruits, this bread can be braided with three, four, five, or six ropes. Yields 1 loaf.

Ingredients

¾ cup	warm water (105°–115°F)
½ cup	sourdough starter (p. 12)
4–4½ cups	flour
1 stick	unsalted butter
½ cup	sugar
2	egg yolks
1 teaspoon	salt
½ teaspoon	ground cinnamon
¼ teaspoon	grated nutmeg
½ teaspoon	grated lemon peel
⅔ cup	sliced almonds
⅓ cup	golden raisins
⅓ cup	chopped candied red cherries
⅓ cup	chopped candied green cherries

Preparation

1 Combine warm water, sourdough starter, and 2 cups flour in mixing bowl. Cover; leave on counter overnight at room temperature.

2 Next day, cream butter, sugar, and egg yolks together. Add 1 cup flour, salt, cinnamon, nutmeg, and lemon peel. Combine this mixture with sourdough mixture. Mix thoroughly.

3 Stir in almonds, raisins, and cherries. Add enough remaining flour to make a soft dough.

4 Knead on lightly floured surface until smooth—about 10 minutes.

5 Divide dough into thirds and roll each into 20-inch rope. Braid and place on greased baking sheet.

6 Let rise in warm place until double—about 1 hour. Bake in a preheated 350°F oven 50–60 minutes or until done. Cool on wire rack.

Festive Braid

Simple and quicker to make than most festive breads, this braid will brighten any Christmas celebration. Yields 1 loaf.

Ingredients

2½–3 cups	flour
1 tablespoon	active dry yeast
⅓ cup	milk
⅓ cup	water
6 tablespoons	unsalted butter
⅓ cup	sugar
½ teaspoon	salt
½ teaspoon	grated orange peel
¼ teaspoon	ground cardamom
1	egg
½ cup	chopped mixed candied fruit

Preparation

1 Combine 1½ cups flour and yeast in mixing bowl. Heat milk, water, butter, sugar, salt, orange peel, and cardamom to hot (120°–130°F).

2 Add milk mixture, egg, and candied fruit to flour mixture.

3 Add enough remaining flour to make a soft dough. Knead on lightly floured surface until smooth—about 10 minutes.

4 Cover dough with bowl and let rest 20 minutes.

5 Divide dough into 3 equal pieces, make ropes, and braid. Pinch ends, and place on greased baking sheet. Cover; let rise in warm place until double—about 30–45 minutes.

6 Bake in a preheated 375°F oven about 30–40 minutes or until done. Cool on wire rack.

Chapter 19

Festive Breads for Other Occasions

*T*he holidays covered in the preceding chapters are only a sampling of the days set aside throughout the world for rejoicing. In most nations a national holiday leads off the nonreligious holidays. The Roman Catholic Church lists fifty-eight saints with feast days, and numerous other saints are celebrated locally. Such holidays as the Oktoberfest, Tulip Festival, Cherry Viewing, and many other regional holidays could have their distinctive breads.

*T*his chapter is a potpourri of holiday breads useful for any festive occasion. Some are fancy, some simple. Some are exotic, some of American origin. Several undoubtedly were once attached to a particular holiday—but you can bake them on the holiday of your choice (or even your making).

*I*n fact, why not create a celebration by treating family or friends to one of these gourmet breads on some occasion that is not a formal holiday?

Welsh Currant Bread

Bara Brith, as this fragrant bread is called in Wales, literally means "currant bread." Yields 1 loaf.

Ingredients

2–2½ cups	flour
⅓ cup	light brown sugar, firmly packed
½ tablespoon	active dry yeast
½ teaspoon	salt
½ teaspoon	ground allspice
3 tablespoons	unsalted butter, softened
½ cup	hot water (120°–130°F)
¼ cup	golden raisins
¼ cup	currants
¼ cup	chopped candied orange peel
1	egg
	honey, if desired

Preparation

1 Combine 1 cup flour, sugar, yeast, salt, allspice, and butter in a mixing bowl. Add hot water; mix thoroughly.

2 Stir in raisins, currants, candied orange peel, and egg. Stir in remaining flour to make a soft dough.

3 Knead on lightly floured surface until smooth—about 10 minutes.

4 Place in greased bowl, turning to coat top. Cover; let rise in warm place until double—about 1 hour.

5 Punch down dough. Shape and place in greased 4 x 8-inch loaf pan.

6 Cover; let rise until dough is about 1 inch above the top of pan—about 30–45 minutes.

7 Bake in a preheated 350°F oven about 50–60 minutes or until done. Cool on wire rack.

8 If desired, dip brush in honey and brush top of loaf.

Oatmeal Bannock

For centuries, the Scots have served different kinds of bannock on various holidays and special occasions. Here's a version featuring oatmeal. Yields 1 loaf.

Ingredients

1–2 cups	flour
3 tablespoons	sugar
½ teaspoon	salt
½ cup	old-fashioned oats
1 tablespoon	active dry yeast
¼ cup	milk
¼ cup	water
4 tablespoons	unsalted butter
1	egg
¼ cup	currants

Preparation

1 Combine 1 cup flour, sugar, salt, oats, and yeast in a mixing bowl. Heat milk, water, and butter to hot (120°–130°F).

2 Add milk mixture to dry ingredients. Mix thoroughly. Add egg and enough remaining flour to make a soft dough.

3 Knead on lightly floured surface until smooth—about 10 minutes.

4 Place in greased bowl, turning to coat top. Cover; let rise in warm place until double—about 1 hour.

5 Punch down dough. Knead in currants.

6 Roll into an 8-inch circle. Place in greased 8-inch cake pan. Use sharp knife to mark circle into 8 wedges, cutting almost to bottom.

7 Cover; let rise in warm place until double—about 30 minutes.

8 Bake in a preheated 375°F oven 20–25 minutes or until done. Cool on wire rack.

Italian Almond Braid

This Italian treat (braid or wreath) is appropriate at Christmas—or any other festive occasion. For almond-lovers especially, but a universal favorite. Yields 1 loaf.

Ingredients

½ tablespoon	active dry yeast
¼ cup	warm water (105°–115°F)
6 tablespoons	unsalted butter, softened
2 tablespoons	sugar
1	egg
¼ teaspoon	salt
½ teaspoon	almond extract
2–2½ cups	flour

Topping

¼ cup	almond paste (p. 215)
1	egg white
1 tablespoon	sugar

Preparation

1 Dissolve yeast in warm water. Set aside for 5 minutes. Combine butter, sugar, egg, salt, and almond extract in mixing bowl. Mix thoroughly.

2 Add 1½ cups flour and yeast mixture to butter mixture. Mix thoroughly.

3 Add enough remaining flour to make a soft dough. Knead on lightly floured surface until smooth—about 10 minutes.

4 Place in greased bowl, turning to coat top. Cover; let rise in warm place until double—about 1 hour.

5 Punch down dough. Using mixer, beat almond paste, egg white, and sugar until smooth. Divide into 3 equal pieces and braid.

6 Place on greased baking sheet. Brush the topping on braid. Let rise in warm place until double—about 30 minutes.

7 Bake in a preheated 350°F oven about 25–30 minutes or until done. Cool on wire rack.

Wreath

Using same recipe, shape into wreath.
(a) Divide into 3 equal pieces. Roll into ropes; braid and place on greased baking sheet. Form into a circle. Pinch ends together.

(b) Shape dough into ball. Stretch dough to form a 4-inch hole in center. Place on greased baking sheet. Put greased custard dish in hole to hold shape.

Buccellati (boo-chay-LAH-tee)

This ring-shaped bread flavored with sweet wine is another favorite from Italy. Just savor its accents of lemon and anise! Yields 1 ring.

Ingredients

½ tablespoon	active dry yeast
2 tablespoons	warm water (105°–115°F)
1½–2 cups	flour
3 tablespoons	unsalted butter, softened
3 tablespoons	sugar
1	egg
1 teaspoon	aniseeds
1 teaspoon	grated lemon peel
1 tablespoon	Marsala or Port
¼ teaspoon	salt
3 tablespoons	chopped candied lemon peel
Glaze	
1	egg white, beaten with 1 tablespoon water

Preparation

1 Dissolve yeast in warm water. Set aside for 5 minutes.

2 Combine 1 cup flour, butter, sugar, egg, aniseeds, grated lemon peel, wine, and salt in mixing bowl. Mix thoroughly.

3 Add yeast mixture. Mix thoroughly. Add enough remaining flour to make a soft dough.

4 Knead on lightly floured surface until smooth—about 10 minutes. Place in greased bowl, turning to coat top.

5 Cover; let rise in warm place until double—about 1 hour.

6 Knead in candied lemon peel. Let rest for 10 minutes.

7 Shape into round ball. Stretch dough to form a 4-inch hole in center. Place ring on greased baking sheet. Put greased custard dish in hole to hold shape.

8 Cover; let rise until double—about 30 minutes. Make glaze and brush on loaf. Bake in a preheated 375°F oven 30–40 minutes or until done.

9 Cool on wire rack.

Pepper Bread

Going back to the Middle Ages, this Italian bread offers a traditional combination of hot and sweet—mingling pepper with dates and, if you wish, chocolate. I find that the delicate warmth it leaves in the mouth is part of its unique charm. Yields 1 loaf.

Ingredients

⅓ cup	dark raisins
½ cup	warm water
⅓ cup	chopped walnuts
⅓ cup	chopped almonds
⅓ cup	chopped pitted dates
⅓ cup	chopped mixed candied fruit
3½–4 cups	flour
1 tablespoon	active dry yeast
½ teaspoon	salt
1 teaspoon	black pepper (preferably freshly ground)
½ teaspoon	grated nutmeg
½ teaspoon	ground cinnamon
2 tablespoons	olive oil
¾ cup	hot water (120°–130°F)
1	egg
⅓ cup	honey
⅓ cup	chocolate chips, if desired

Preparation

1 Soak raisins in warm water for 10 minutes. Then drain and dry. Combine raisins, walnuts, almonds, dates, and candied fruit in mixing bowl.

2 Combine 2 cups flour, yeast, salt, pepper, nutmeg, and cinnamon in large bowl.

3 Add oil, hot water, egg, honey, and nuts and fruit mixture. Mix thoroughly.

4 Add enough remaining flour to make a soft dough. Knead on lightly floured surface until smooth—about 10 minutes.

5 Place in greased bowl, turning to coat top. Cover; let rise in warm place until double—about 1½ hours.

6 Punch down dough. Knead in chocolate chips if using them. Let rest; cover with inverted bowl for 10 minutes.

7 Shape into a round loaf. Place in greased 2-quart soufflé dish.

8 Cover; let rise until dough reaches top of soufflé dish.

9 Bake in a preheated 350°F oven for 45–55 minutes or until done. Cool on wire rack.

Greek Holiday Loaf

This holiday bread is served in Greece at Christmas with walnut decorations and at Easter with red hard-cooked eggs baked on it. A treat any time. Yields 1 loaf.

Ingredients

1 tablespoon	active dry yeast
⅓ cup	warm milk (105°–115°F)
1 stick	unsalted butter
1 cup	sugar
4	eggs
1	egg yolk
1 medium	boiled potato, mashed*
3–3½ cups	flour
1	beaten egg yolk
	hard-cooked eggs, dyed red, if desired
	walnuts, if desired
	candied cherries, if desired

Preparation

1 Dissolve yeast in warm milk. Set aside for 5 minutes. Mix butter and sugar in a large bowl. Add eggs and egg yolk. Mix thoroughly.

2 Add yeast mixture to sugar mixture. Add potato and enough flour to make a soft dough.

3 Knead on lightly floured surface until smooth—about 10 minutes.

4 Place in greased bowl, turning to coat top. Cover; let rise in warm place until double—about 1 hour.

5 Punch down dough. Shape into loaf and place in greased 9 x 5-inch loaf pan.

6 Cover; let rise until double—about 45 minutes.

7 Brush top with beaten egg yolk. (At Eastertime, garnish with dyed eggs; at Christmas, garnish with walnuts and candied cherries.) Bake in a preheated 350°F oven 45–60 minutes or until done. Cool on wire rack.

*If potato has been salted, omit salt from recipe. Otherwise add ½ teaspoon salt.

Kouloura (coo-LOO-ra)

In Greece, hard-cooked eggs are sometimes pushed into this bread fresh from the oven to make an Easter kouloura. But the bread is also enjoyed on other festive occasions. Yields 1 loaf.

Ingredients

2½—3 cups	flour
½ tablespoon	active dry yeast
¼ teaspoon	ground cinnamon
¼ cup	milk
¼ cup	water
2 tablespoons	unsalted butter, melted
¼ cup	sugar
¼ teaspoon	salt
1	egg
	sesame seeds

Glaze

1 tablespoon	water beaten with
1	egg yolk

Preparation

1 Combine 2 cups flour, yeast, and cinnamon in mixing bowl. Heat milk, water, butter, sugar, and salt to hot (120°–130°F).

2 Add milk mixture and egg to dry ingredients. Mix thoroughly. Add enough remaining flour to make a soft dough. Knead on lightly floured surface until smooth—about 10 minutes.

3 Place in greased bowl, turning to coat top. Cover; let rise in warm place until double—about 1 hour.

4 Punch down dough. Shape dough into ball; place in greased 8-inch round pan.

5 Cover; let rise in warm place until double.

6 Make glaze and brush on loaf. Sprinkle with sesame seeds. Bake in a preheated 350°F oven 30 minutes or until done. Cool on wire rack.

Greek Braid

A handsome bread, delicately flavored with anise and sesame seeds, Greek Braid has a versatility that you'll find suitable for many special occasions. Yields 1 braid.

Ingredients

2–2½ cups	flour	
½ tablespoon	active dry yeast	
⅓ cup	water	
3 tablespoons	nonfat dry milk	
½ teaspoon	ground aniseeds	
3 tablespoons	unsalted butter	
3 tablespoons	sugar	
¼ teaspoon	salt	
1	egg	

Topping

1	egg	
1 tablespoon	milk	
2 tablespoons	chopped almonds	
2 tablespoons	sesame seeds	
2 tablespoons	sugar	

Preparation

1   Combine 1½ cups flour and yeast. Heat water, dry milk, aniseeds, butter, sugar, and salt to hot (120°–130°F). Add to flour mixture and mix thoroughly.

2   Add egg and enough remaining flour to make a soft dough. Knead on lightly floured surface until smooth—about 10 minutes.

3   Place in greased bowl, turning to coat top. Cover; let rise in warm place until double—about 1 hour.

4   Punch down dough. Divide in thirds; make each into 16-inch rope. Braid.

5   Place on greased baking sheet. Cover; let rise in warm place 30 minutes.

6   Mix egg and milk thoroughly. Brush over top of braid. Sprinkle with almonds and sesame seeds, then sugar. Bake in a preheated 350°F oven 30–40 minutes or until done. Cool on wire rack.

Kolachy (ko-LAH-chee)

Bohemian kolachy (or "wheel"), is a treat in itself, and you can vary it with the four delicious fillings included below. Yields 15 buns.

Ingredients

1 tablespoon	active dry yeast
⅓ cup	warm water (105°–115°F)
2–2½ cups	flour
3 tablespoons	sugar
½ teaspoon	salt
¼ teaspoon	ground mace
½ teaspoon	grated lemon peel
4 tablespoons	unsalted butter
⅓ cup	warm milk (105°–115°F)
1	egg
Glaze	
1	egg yolk
1 tablespoon	water

Preparation

1 Dissolve yeast in warm water. Set aside for 5 minutes. Combine 1½ cups flour, sugar, salt, mace, lemon peel, and butter in mixing bowl. Mix thoroughly.

2 Add yeast mixture, warm milk, and egg. Mix thoroughly.

3 Add enough remaining flour to make a soft dough. Knead on lightly floured surface until smooth—about 10 minutes.

4 Place in greased bowl, turning to coat top. Cover; let rise in warm place until double—about 1 hour.

5 Punch down dough. Let rise again until double—about 30 minutes.

6 Prepare any of the fillings below. After dough rises, shape dough into (a) squares or (b) ovals.
(a) Squares: Cut into 3-inch squares. Put 1 heaping teaspoon of filling on each. Fold corners into center and press firmly.
(b) Ovals: Roll balls of dough into ovals. Place 1 heaping teaspoon of filling on one side of each. Fold other side over. Pinch edges together tightly.

7 Place on greased baking sheet. Let rise until not quite double—about 15 minutes. Make glaze and brush on loaf.

8 Bake in a preheated 350°F oven 15–18 minutes or until done. Cool on wire rack.

Fillings

Poppy Seed-Fruit

12	prunes or dried apricots, mashed	
¼ teaspoon	ground cinnamon	
1 tablespoon	sugar	
1 tablespoon	poppy seeds	

- Cover prunes or apricots with water and cook until tender. Drain and mash with fork. Add cinnamon, sugar, and poppy seeds. Mix thoroughly. Filling will be thick.

Prune

12	prunes
2 tablespoons	sugar
¼ teaspoon	ground allspice

- Cover prunes with water and cook until tender. Drain and mash with fork. Add sugar and allspice. Filling will be thick.

Apricot

24	dried apricots
¼ cup	sugar

- Cover apricots with water and cook until tender. Drain. Mix in blender until smooth. Add sugar. Mix thoroughly. Filling will be thick.

Prune-Apricot

6	prunes
12	dried apricots
2 tablespoons	sugar
1 tablespoon	orange juice
½ tablespoon	grated orange peel

- Cover prunes and apricots with water and cook until tender. Drain. Mix in blender until smooth. Add sugar, orange juice, and orange peel. Filling will be thick.

Yugoslavian Holiday Bread

The people in southern Yugoslavia bake this fragrant,
walnut-filled bread for festive occasions. Try a loaf at your next
coffee klatch. Yields 1 loaf.

Ingredients

2–3 cups	flour
3 tablespoons	sugar
½ teaspoon	salt
½ tablespoon	active dry yeast
2 tablespoons	unsalted butter, softened
1 medium	egg
⅓ cup	hot water (120°–130°F)
½ teaspoon	grated orange peel
	warm, clear honey, if preferred
	walnut halves
	candied cherry halves

Filling

2 tablespoons	unsalted butter, softened
¼ cup	light brown sugar, firmly packed
1 medium	egg
½ teaspoon	grated orange peel
¾ cup	chopped walnuts

Preparation

1 Combine 1 cup flour, sugar, salt, and yeast in mixing bowl. Add butter, egg, hot water, and orange peel. Mix thoroughly.

2 Add enough remaining flour to make a soft dough.

3 Knead on lightly floured surface until smooth—about 10 minutes. Place in greased bowl, turning to coat top.

4 Cover; let rise in warm place until double—about 1 hour. Make filling.

5 Punch down dough. Let rest 10 minutes. Roll to a 7 x 10-inch rectangle.

6 Spread filling evenly, leaving 1-inch margin. Roll up jelly-roll style; pinch to seal.

7 Form into a snail shape (coil) on large greased baking sheet. Cover; let rise in warm place until double—about 30–45 minutes.

8 Bake in a preheated 350°F oven 30–40 minutes or until done. Cool on wire rack.

Frosting

1 tablespoon	unsalted butter, melted
½ cup	confectioners' sugar
½–1 tablespoon	milk
¼ teaspoon	orange extract

9 Make frosting and spread on top or, if preferred, spread top with 3 tablespoons warm, clear honey. Decorate with walnut halves and candied cherry halves.

Czech Poppy Seed Loaf

For a bread that is festive but light it would be hard to beat this charming Czechoslovakian loaf. Note that you aren't supposed to knead this bread. Yields 1 loaf.

Ingredients

½ tablespoon	active dry yeast
2 tablespoons	warm water (105°–115°F)
¾ cup	unsalted butter
5	egg yolks
1 teaspoon	grated lemon peel
1 teaspoon	lemon juice
¼ teaspoon	salt
2–2½ cups	flour
⅓ cup	warm heavy cream (105°–115°F)
⅓ cup	chopped almonds
½ cup	poppy seeds
⅓ cup	light brown sugar, firmly packed
4	egg whites
1 teaspoon	almond extract
	confectioners' sugar

Preparation

1 Dissolve yeast in warm water. Set aside for 5 minutes. Using a mixer, cream together butter and egg yolks. Add lemon peel, lemon juice, and salt.

2 Add 1½ cups flour, warm cream, almonds, poppy seeds, and brown sugar. Mix. Beat egg whites until stiff. Add almond extract.

3 Add yeast mixture to butter mixture. Gradually add egg whites. Add enough remaining flour to make a soft dough. Beat until light and stiff. No kneading is necessary.

4 Place in greased 6-cup Bundt pan. Cover; let rise until double—about 30 minutes (an inch from top of pan).

5 Bake in a preheated 375°F oven 40 minutes or until done. Cool in pan about 15 minutes. Cool on wire rack. Sprinkle with confectioners' sugar.

Nisu (NIH-SOO)

From Finland, nisu is one of the more delicate of festive breads, scented with cardamom. Try this when you want something tasty but not too assertive for your holiday celebration. Yields 1 loaf.

Ingredients

1–2 cups	flour
½ tablespoon	active dry yeast
¼ cup	nonfat dry milk
½ teaspoon	salt
2 tablespoons	sugar
⅓ cup	hot water (120°–130°F)
1 tablespoon	unsalted butter, softened
1	egg
½ teaspoon	ground cardamom

Glaze

1	egg yolk, beaten with 1 tablespoon milk

Preparation

1 Combine 1 cup flour, yeast, dry milk, salt, sugar, and hot water in mixing bowl. Add butter, egg, and cardamom. Mix thoroughly.

2 Add enough remaining flour to make a soft dough. Knead on lightly floured surface until smooth—about 10 minutes.

3 Place in greased bowl, turning to coat top. Cover; let rise in warm place until double—about 1 hour.

4 Punch down dough. Divide dough into thirds, making 3 ropes. Braid. Place in greased 5 x 9-inch loaf pan.

5 Cover; let rise in warm place until double—about 30 minutes.

6 Make glaze and brush on loaf. Bake in a preheated 350°F oven 30–40 minutes or until done. Cool on wire rack.

Krendl (KREHN-del)

In Russia, this pretzel-shaped bread traditionally has been a feature of anniversaries and other ceremonial parties. Your friends will adore its distinctive shape and delectable fruit filling. Yields 1 loaf.

Ingredients

½ tablespoon	active dry yeast
2 tablespoons	warm water (105°–115°F)
½ cup	milk
2 tablespoons	unsalted butter
1 tablespoon	sugar
¼ teaspoon	salt
3–3½ cups	flour
½ teaspoon	vanilla extract
2	egg yolks
	Confectioners' Icing (p. 208)
	sliced almonds

Filling

3	Delicious apples
1 tablespoon	unsalted butter
2 tablespoons	sugar
½ cup	chopped prunes
½ cup	chopped dried apricots
	unsalted butter, melted

Preparation

1 Dissolve yeast in warm water. Set aside for 5 minutes. Heat milk, butter, sugar, and salt to warm (105°–115°F).

2 Combine 2 cups flour, vanilla, and egg yolks in mixing bowl. Mix thoroughly. Add yeast mixture, milk mixture, and enough remaining flour to make a soft dough. Mix thoroughly.

3 Knead on lightly floured surface until smooth—about 10 minutes. Place in greased bowl, turning to coat top.

4 Cover; let rise in warm place until double—about 1 hour. While dough is rising, prepare filling.

5 Peel, core, and slice apples thin. Heat butter and sugar. Add apples and cook over medium heat until tender, stirring constantly. Add prunes and apricots, and remove from heat.

6 Punch down dough. Roll into a 10 x 30-inch rectangle. Spread with melted butter. Combine sugar and cinnamon. Sprinkle mixture on dough.

7 Spread filling evenly. Starting with wider side, roll up jelly-roll style. Pinch seams and edges.

8 Form into pretzel-shape. (See drawing, page 195.) Place on a greased baking sheet. Tuck ends under center of dough; flatten slightly.

9 Cover; let rise in warm place until double—about 30 minutes. Bake in a preheated 350°F oven about 45–60 minutes or until done.

2 tablespoons   sugar

½ teaspoon   ground cinnamon

10 Cool slightly. Frost with Confectioners' Icing and sprinkle with almonds. Cool on wire rack.

Danish Twist

Here's a twist from Denmark, dotted with almonds, that really hits the spot with coffee on any festive occasion. Yields 1 cake.

Ingredients

½ tablespoon	active dry yeast
2 tablespoons	warm water (105°–115°F)
½ cup	milk
4 tablespoons	light brown sugar, firmly packed
¼ teaspoon	salt
4 tablespoons	unsalted butter
1½–2 cups	flour
1 teaspoon	ground cardamom
2	egg yolks
	Confectioners' Icing (p. 208)
	sliced almonds

Glaze

1	egg, beaten with 1 tablespoon water

Preparation

1 Dissolve yeast in warm water. Set aside for 5 minutes. Heat milk, brown sugar, salt, and butter to warm (105°–115°F).

2 Combine 1½ cups flour, cardamom, yeast mixture, and milk mixture in large bowl. Add egg yolks, and mix thoroughly.

3 Add enough remaining flour to make a soft dough. Knead on lightly floured surface until smooth—about 10 minutes.

4 Place in greased bowl, turning to coat top. Cover; let rise in warm place until double—about 1 hour.

5 Punch down dough. Divide dough in half, make 2 ropes about 18 inches long, and twist.

6 Place on greased baking sheet. Make glaze and brush on loaf. Cover; let rise in warm place until double—about 30 minutes.

7 Bake in a preheated 350°F oven about 40 minutes or until done. Cool on wire rack.

8 Make Confectioners' Icing and drizzle on twist. Decorate with sliced almonds.

Finnish Potato Rye and Challah, pages 135 and 200 ▶

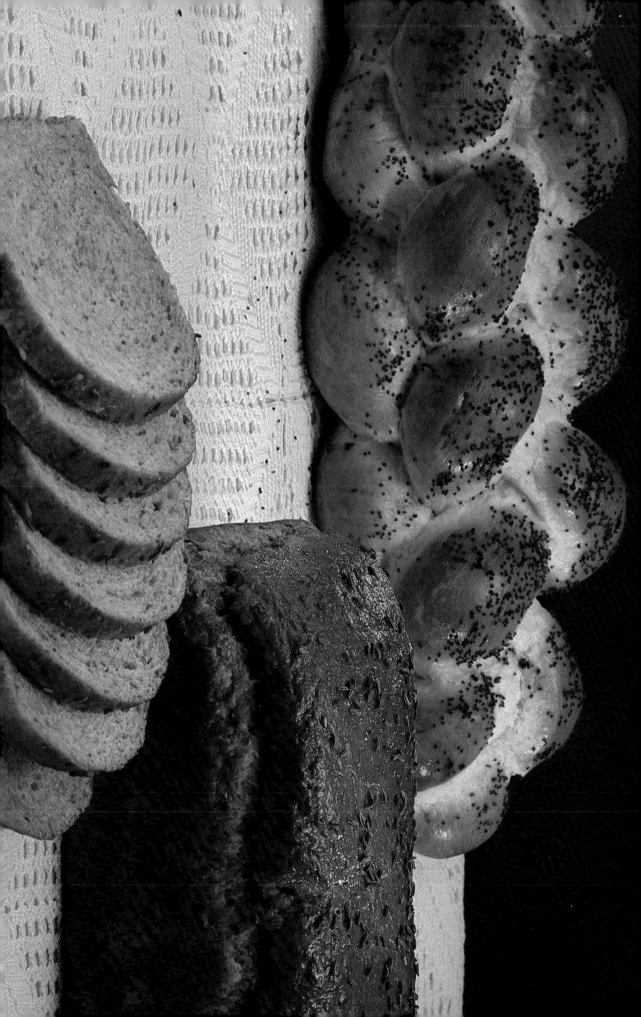

Rose Water Buns

The fragrance of roses makes these buns a special treat,
something that will lift your festivities out of the ordinary.
Yields 12 buns.

Ingredients

1½–2 cups	flour
½ tablespoon	active dry yeast
¼ cup	sugar
1 teaspoon	aniseeds
½ teaspoon	salt
⅓ cup	milk
4 tablespoons	unsalted butter
1	egg

Rose Water Syrup

¼ cup	sugar
2 tablespoons	milk
1 tablespoon	unsalted butter
1 teaspoon	rose water*

Preparation

1 Combine 1 cup flour, yeast, sugar, aniseeds, and salt. Heat milk and butter to hot (120°–130°F). Pour over dry ingredients; mix thoroughly.

2 Add egg, and enough remaining flour to make a soft dough.

3 Knead on lightly floured surface until smooth—about 10 minutes. Place in greased bowl, turning to coat top.

4 Cover; let rise in warm place until double—about 1 hour.

5 Punch down dough. Divide into 12 equal pieces. Cover; let rest for 10 minutes.

6 Make circles about 3 inches in diameter and ¼ inch thick. Place on lightly greased baking sheet.

7 Cover; let rise in warm place until double—about 30 minutes.

8 Bake in a preheated 350°F oven 15–20 minutes or until done. Cool on wire rack.

9 Combine sugar, milk, butter, and rose water in saucepan. Let boil for 4 minutes. With fork, dip each bun into the hot syrup, coating completely. Place on wire rack with waxed paper under it for easy cleaning.

*Rose water may be found in some gourmet shops, pharmacies, and suppliers of Middle Eastern foods.

Mexican Holiday Bread

This gaily festive bread, with its nuts and candied fruits, will add a Latin touch to your celebration. Yields 1 loaf.

Ingredients

1 tablespoon	active dry yeast
¼ cup	warm water (105°–115°F)
⅓ cup	milk
3 tablespoons	unsalted butter
3 tablespoons	sugar
½ teaspoon	salt
3½–4 cups	flour
2	eggs
½ tablespoon	grated orange peel
⅓ cup	chopped candied red cherries
⅓ cup	chopped candied green cherries
⅓ cup	chopped pecans
	Confectioners' Icing (p. 208)
	pecan halves
	candied cherry halves

Preparation

1 Dissolve yeast in warm water. Set aside for 5 minutes. Heat milk, butter, sugar, and salt to warm (105°–115°F).

2 Combine 2 cups flour, yeast mixture, milk mixture, eggs, and orange peel in mixing bowl. Mix thoroughly.

3 Add chopped cherries and nuts and enough remaining flour to make a soft dough. Knead on lightly floured surface until smooth—about 10 minutes.

4 Place in greased bowl, turning to coat top. Cover; let rise in warm place until double—about 1 hour.

5 Punch down dough. Cover; let rest 10 minutes.

6 Form a 22-inch roll and make ring by pinching ends together. Place on greased baking sheet. Cover; let rise until double—about 30 minutes.

7 Bake in a preheated 350°F oven 30 minutes or until done. Cool on wire rack.

8 Drizzle with icing, and decorate with pecans and cherries.

Fruited Buns

These spicy buns make excellent individual treats for guests at a party, especially when a buffet is served. Yields 12 buns.

Ingredients

½ tablespoon	active dry yeast
3 tablespoons	warm water (105°–115°F)
½ cup	milk
2 tablespoons	unsalted butter
¼ teaspoon	salt
¼ cup	sugar
2–2½ cups	flour
¼ teaspoon	ground cinnamon
¼ teaspoon	grated nutmeg
½ teaspoon	ground mace
1	egg
⅓ cup	golden raisins
⅓ cup	chopped walnuts or pecans
¼ cup	chopped mixed candied fruit

Preparation

1 Dissolve yeast in warm water. Set aside for 5 minutes. Heat milk, butter, salt, and sugar to warm (105°–115°F).

2 Combine 1½ cups flour, spices, yeast mixture, and milk mixture. Mix thoroughly.

3 Add egg and enough remaining flour to make a soft dough. Knead in raisins, nuts, and candied fruit. Knead on lightly floured surface until smooth—about 10 minutes.

4 Place in greased bowl, turning to coat top. Cover; let rise in warm place until double—about 1 hour.

5 Punch down dough. Divide dough into 12 equal pieces. Place on greased baking sheet. Cover; let rise in warm place for about 30 minutes or until double.

6 Bake in a preheated 375°F oven for 20 minutes or until done. Cool on wire rack.

Challah (KHAH-luh)

Challah, a braided white bread, is usually eaten on the Sabbath and on many Jewish holidays. But apart from its religious associations, you will find that it goes remarkably well with almost any meal. Yields 1 loaf.

Ingredients

½ tablespoon	active dry yeast
½ cup	warm water (105°–115°F)
1½–2½ cups	flour
1 tablespoon	sugar
½ teaspoon	salt
1 tablespoon	vegetable oil
1	egg

Glaze

1	egg yolk
1½ tablespoons	poppy seeds

Preparation

1. Dissolve yeast in warm water. Set aside for 5 minutes.

2. Combine 1 cup flour, sugar, and salt in mixing bowl. Add yeast mixture, vegetable oil, and egg. Mix thoroughly.

3. Add enough remaining flour to make a soft dough. Knead on lightly floured surface until smooth—about 10 minutes.

4. Place in greased bowl, turning to coat top. Cover; let rise in warm place until double—about 1 hour.

5. Punch down dough. Divide dough into thirds, making 3 ropes, and braid.* Place on greased baking sheet.

6. Cover; let rise in warm place until it is double—about 30–45 minutes.

7. Brush with egg yolk and sprinkle with poppy seeds. Bake in a pre-heated 350°F oven 45–60 minutes or until done. Cool on wire rack.

*You can also braid with four, five, or six ropes.

200

Easy Holiday Bread

No kneading (an exception to the rule) is required in this cheerful-looking holiday treat. Just mix, put in loaf pan, and let rise before baking. Yields 1 loaf.

Ingredients

3–3½ cups	flour
1 tablespoon	active dry yeast
1 cup	milk
4 tablespoons	unsalted butter
¼ cup	sugar
1 teaspoon	salt
1	egg
½ cup	chopped candied red cherries
½ cup	chopped candied green cherries
½ cup	golden raisins

Preparation

1 Combine 1 cup flour and yeast in large mixing bowl.

2 Heat milk, butter, sugar, and salt to hot (120°–130°F). Add milk mixture and egg to flour mixture. Mix thoroughly.

3 Add cherries and raisins. Add enough remaining flour to make a stiff batter.

4 Grease 5 x 9-inch loaf pan or soufflé dish. Pour batter into pan. Cover; let rise in warm place until double—about 1 hour.

5 Bake in a preheated 350°F oven about 50–60 minutes or until done. Cool on wire rack.

CoolRise©* Holiday Bread

The CoolRise© Method, originated by Consumer Kitchens, Robin Hood Flour, allows you to shape bread and then leave it in the refrigerator for 2 to 24 hours—a big help in a tight holiday schedule. Yields 1 loaf.

Ingredients

⅓ cup	milk
3 tablespoons	sugar
½ teaspoon	salt
3 tablespoons	unsalted butter
½ tablespoon	active dry yeast
¼ cup	warm water (105°–115°F)
2–3 cups	flour
1	egg
½ cup	chopped mixed candied fruit
¼ cup	nuts

Preparation

1 Heat milk, sugar, salt, and butter to warm (105°–115°F).

2 Dissolve yeast in warm water. Set aside for 5 minutes. Combine 1½ cups flour, milk mixture, egg, and yeast mixture. Mix thoroughly. Add candied fruit and nuts.

3 Add enough remaining flour to make a soft dough. Knead on lightly floured surface until smooth—about 10 minutes.

4 Cover; let rise in warm place until double—about 1 hour.

5 Punch down dough. Shape into loaf and place in greased 9 x 5-inch loaf pan. Cover pan loosely with plastic wrap and damp towel.

6 Refrigerate 2–24 hours. When ready to bake, remove from refrigerator and take off towel and plastic wrap. Let stand 10 minutes.

7 Bake in a preheated 350°F oven 30 minutes or until done. Cool on wire rack.

*Courtesy Robin Hood Flour, International Multifoods.

Holiday Twists

You'll find that this elegant bread, rich with cream, brightens any festive occasion. Also good as a snack with coffee. Yields 12 rolls.

Ingredients

½ tablespoon	active dry yeast
2 tablespoons	warm water (105°–115°F)
¼ cup	dairy sour cream
4 tablespoons	unsalted butter, softened
¼ teaspoon	salt
3 tablespoons	sugar
1–1½ cups	flour
½ teaspoon	grated lemon peel
1	egg
2 tablespoons	chopped candied cherries
2 tablespoons	chopped walnuts
	sugar

Preparation

1 Dissolve yeast in warm water. Set aside for 5 minutes. Heat sour cream, butter, salt, and sugar to warm (105°–115°F).

2 Combine 1 cup flour, lemon peel, yeast mixture, egg, and milk mixture in mixing bowl. Mix thoroughly.

3 Knead in cherries and walnuts. Cover; place in refrigerator 2–24 hours.

4 Sprinkle surface lightly with sugar. Roll dough into an 8 x 12-inch rectangle. Sprinkle dough lightly with sugar. Fold dough from 2 opposite sides, making 3 layers. Repeat twice.

5 Roll into an 8 x 12-inch rectangle. Cut into strips 4 inches long and 1 inch wide. Holding up, twist strips 3 or 4 times. Place 1 inch apart on greased baking sheet.

6 Bake in a preheated 375°F oven 15–20 minutes or until done. Cool on wire rack.

Sourdough Strawberry Braid

Strawberry preserves give this bread zip. You'll find it a fascinating change of pace from other holiday breads. Yields 1 loaf.

Ingredients

1 tablespoon	active dry yeast
½ cup	warm water (105°–115°F)
½ cup	sourdough starter (p. 12)
4–5 cups	flour
¼ cup	sugar
4 tablespoons	unsalted butter, melted
¾ teaspoon	salt
1	egg
⅔ cup	strawberry or other preserves
	Confectioners' Icing (p. 208), if desired

Preparation

1 Dissolve yeast in warm water. Set aside for 5 minutes. Add ½ cup sourdough starter and 1 cup flour. Mix thoroughly. Let stand 8 hours or overnight.

2 Stir to dissolve crust that has formed on top of the starter. Add 2 cups flour, sugar, butter, salt, and egg. Mix thoroughly.

3 Add enough remaining flour to make a soft dough. Knead on lightly floured surface until smooth—about 10 minutes.

4 Place in greased bowl, turning to coat top. Cover; let rise in warm place until double—about 1 hour.

5 Punch down dough. Make a 9-inch square. Put preserves down the middle third. With scissors, cut strips toward center 3 inches long and 1 inch wide. Alternating sides, fold strips over filling. Place on greased baking sheet.

6 Cover; let rise until almost double—about 30 minutes.

7 Bake in a preheated 375°F oven 30–40 minutes or until done.

8 Cool on wire rack. If desired, drizzle with Confectioners' Icing.

Party Braid

Shaped like the Sourdough Strawberry Braid, this bread is filled with the goodies we all enjoy. Rich, cheerful, and filling! Yields 1 loaf.

Ingredients

½ tablespoon	active dry yeast	
2 tablespoons	warm water (105°–115°F)	
3 tablespoons	milk	
3 tablespoons	unsalted butter	
3 tablespoons	sugar	
¼ teaspoon	salt	
2–2½ cups	flour	
½ teaspoon	ground cardamom	
1	grated orange peel	
1	egg	
	Confectioners' Icing (p. 208), if desired	

Filling

¼ cup	chopped dates	
2 tablespoons	light brown sugar, firmly packed	
¼ cup	chopped pecans	
2 tablespoons	maraschino cherries	
2 tablespoons	shredded coconut, if desired	

Preparation

1. Dissolve yeast in warm water. Set aside for 5 minutes. Heat milk, butter, sugar, and salt to warm (105°–115°F).

2. Combine 1½ cups flour, cardamom, orange peel, yeast mixture, and milk mixture in large bowl. Mix thoroughly.

3. Add egg and enough remaining flour to make a soft dough. Knead on lightly floured surface until smooth—about 10 minutes.

4. Place in greased bowl, turning to coat top. Cover; let rise in warm place until double—about 1 hour.

5. Punch down dough. Knead about 3 minutes. Combine all ingredients for filling.

6. Make a 9-inch square. Put filling down the middle third. With scissors, cut strips toward center 3 inches long and 1 inch wide. Alternating sides, fold strips over filling. Place on greased baking sheet.

7. Cover; let rise in warm place until double—about 30 minutes.

8. Bake in a preheated 350°F oven 30 minutes or until done. Cool on wire rack. If desired, drizzle with Confectioners' Icing.

Holiday Sweet Bread

Potato adds body to this unusual sweet bread enhanced with raisins and mixed candied fruit. Yields 1 loaf.

Ingredients

2–2½ cups	flour
½ tablespoon	active dry yeast
½ teaspoon	grated lemon peel
½ cup	potato water
¼ cup	sugar
2 tablespoons	unsalted butter
½ teaspoon	salt
1	egg
⅓ cup	boiled mashed potato, water reserved
⅓ cup	golden raisins
⅔ cup	chopped mixed candied fruit
Glaze	
1	egg, beaten with 1 tablespoon water

Preparation

1 Combine 1½ cups flour, yeast, and lemon peel in mixing bowl. Heat potato water, sugar, butter, and salt to hot (120°–130°F). Add to dry ingredients. Mix thoroughly.

2 Add egg and mashed potato to the dry ingredients. Mix thoroughly.

3 Add raisins, candied fruit, and enough remaining flour to make a soft dough. Knead on lightly floured surface until smooth—about 10 minutes.

4 Place in greased bowl, turning to coat top. Cover; let rise in warm place until double—about 1 hour.

5 Punch down dough. Shape into a ball; place in greased 8-inch round pan.

6 Cover; let rise until double—about 30–45 minutes. Make glaze and brush on loaf.

7 Bake in a preheated 350°F oven 60 minutes or until done. Cool on wire rack.

Contents 20

Icings and Fillings

This chapter describes the extra touches you can add to many holiday breads for greater variety. After reading the following suggestions, let your imagination rove. You can develop exciting ideas of your own!

Icings

1 Before icing, cool bread slightly. Place bread on wire rack. Slip waxed paper under rack. (This makes for easy clean-up.)

2 With spoon, drizzle icing back and forth across loaf.

3 If desired, add nuts or fruits as decorations before icing sets.

Confectioners'

½ cup sifted confectioners' sugar

½ teaspoon vanilla extract

1–2 tablespoons milk

• Mix thoroughly.

Mocha

½ cup sifted confectioners' sugar

½ tablespoon unsalted butter

1–2 teaspoons brewed coffee

• Mix thoroughly.

Chocolate

½-ounce square unsweetened chocolate

½ tablespoon unsalted butter

½ cup sifted confectioners' sugar

½ teaspoon vanilla extract

1½ tablespoons milk

Place chocolate and butter in small saucepan. Stir over low heat. When melted, remove from heat. Add sugar, vanilla, and milk. Mix thoroughly.

Lemon

½ cup sifted confectioners' sugar

1–2 tablespoons milk

1–1½ teaspoons lemon juice

• Mix thoroughly.

Orange

½ cup sifted confectioners' sugar

½ tablespoon unsalted butter

1–2 teaspoons orange juice

½ teaspoon grated orange peel

• Mix thoroughly.

Cinnamon

½ cup sifted confectioners' sugar

1½–2 tablespoons milk

½ teaspoon vanilla extract

¼ teaspoon ground cinnamon

• Mix thoroughly.

Nutmeg

½ cup sifted confectioners' sugar

1–2 tablespoons milk

½ teaspoon vanilla extract

¼ teaspoon grated nutmeg

• Mix thoroughly.

Almond

½ cup sifted confectioners' sugar

1½ tablespoons milk

¼ teaspoon almond extract

• Mix thoroughly.

Mint

½ cup sifted confectioners' sugar

1 tablespoon milk

1–1½ teaspoons crème de menthe

• Mix thoroughly.

Peppermint Stick

½ cup sifted confectioners' sugar

1½–2 tablespoons milk

⅛ teaspoon mint extract

1 teaspoon crushed peppermint candy

- Mix thoroughly.

Pineapple

½ cup sifted confectioners' sugar

1½ tablespoons pineapple juice

- Mix thoroughly.

Try other icings—invent your own!

$\mathcal{F}$illings

Roll dough into rectangle. Brush dough with melted butter before spreading with filling.

Almond—combine 3 cups sifted confectioners' sugar, 2 tablespoons soft unsalted butter, 1½ teaspoons almond extract, ½ cup finely ground almonds, 3 tablespoons heavy cream. Mix thoroughly.

Almond-cherry—combine 1 cup firmly packed light brown sugar, ½ cup chopped almonds, ½ cup chopped maraschino cherries, and 2 teaspoons almond extract. Mix thoroughly.

Almond-coconut—combine 1 cup finely ground almonds, ⅔ cup shredded coconut, and 4 tablespoons soft butter. Mix thoroughly.

Almond paste—combine 7 ounces almond paste (p. 215), 2 egg whites, ⅓ cup sugar, and ⅓ cup finely chopped almonds. Mix thoroughly.

Apple—combine 1 cup thinly sliced pared apples, ½ cup sugar, and 1 teaspoon ground cinnamon. If desired, add ⅓ cup walnuts. Mix thoroughly.

Apple-raisin—combine 2 peeled, finely sliced apples with ½ cup brown sugar, ¼ cup golden raisins, 2½ tablespoons softened butter, and 1 teaspoon grated orange or lemon peel. Mix thoroughly.

Apricot-cherry—combine 1 cup chopped dried apricots and 1 cup finely chopped maraschino cherries. Mix thoroughly.

Candied fruit—combine 1 cup chopped red cherries, 1/4 cup chopped candied pineapple, 1/4 cup chopped candied orange peel, 1/2 cup chopped golden raisins, and 4 tablespoons melted butter. Mix thoroughly.

Cinnamon-sugar—combine 1/2 cup sugar, 1/4 cup shredded coconut, pecans and/or dark raisins, and 1 1/2 teaspoons ground cinnamon. Mix thoroughly.

Coconut-butterscotch—combine 1/2 cup shredded coconut, 1/2 cup walnuts or pecans, and 1/4 cup firmly packed light brown sugar. Add 2 tablespoons melted butter. Mix thoroughly.

Cream cheese—cream 8 ounces softened cream cheese and 1/3 cup sugar until light and fluffy. Blend in 1 egg yolk. Mix thoroughly.

Date-nut—combine in a saucepan 1 cup chopped dates and 3 tablespoons water. Heat to a boil. Lower heat, cover, and simmer about 3 minutes. When water is absorbed, add 1/2 cup chopped walnuts or pecans. Mix thoroughly.

Fig—combine in a saucepan 3/4 cup chopped dried figs, 3 tablespoons light brown sugar, 1/2 cup water, and 4 teaspoons lemon juice. Heat. Stir until thick. When cool, add 1/3 cup chopped walnuts or pecans. Mix thoroughly.

Orange-coconut—combine 1/4 cup sugar, 1/2 cup shredded coconut, and 2 tablespoons grated orange peel. Mix thoroughly.

Orange marmalade-nut—brush dough with melted butter. Spread dough with thin layer of orange marmalade. Sprinkle with finely chopped walnuts or pecans.

Pecan—cream ½ cup butter and ½ cup sugar until light. Add ½ cup chopped pecans and 1 teaspoon ground cinnamon. Mix thoroughly.

Poppy seed—combine in a saucepan 1 cup finely chopped walnuts, ½ cup poppy seeds, ¼ cup honey, 4 tablespoons melted butter, ¼ cup milk, and ¼ cup flour. Heat. Stir until thick. Mix thoroughly. Cool before using.

Prune or apricot—cook 1 cup dried prunes or apricots in water until tender. Drain and purée. Add ⅓ cup sugar and ½ cup water and cook until tender and thick. Mix thoroughly.

Raisin-date—combine 1 cup dark raisins, 1 cup chopped dates, and 1 cup water. Cook together until very soft. If desired, purée while warm. Mix thoroughly. Cool before using.

Walnut-cherry—combine 1 cup chopped walnuts, ½ cup chopped maraschino cherries, and 2 tablespoons sugar. Mix thoroughly.

Almond Paste

You can buy almond paste in gourmet sections of supermarkets. Or you can make your own as follows:

2 cups slivered almonds

2 cups confectioners' sugar

¼ cup water

1 teaspoon almond extract

If you use a blender to grind almonds, put half a cup of almonds in container at a time. Grind almonds until very fine. Continue until all almonds are done. Combine ground almonds with remaining ingredients in large bowl. Use fingers to mix; knead until smooth. Use, or keep in refrigerator or freezer.

If you use a food processor to grind almonds, insert steel blade. Add almonds and process until finely ground. Add remaining ingredients and process until mixture forms a ball. Use, or keep in refrigerator or freezer.

Vanilla Confectioners' Sugar

To make, place half a vanilla bean broken into several pieces in half a cup of sugar. Cover container tightly. Leave at room temperature for 2 or 3 days.

Bibliography

Alston, Elizabeth (ed.), *The Redbook Breadbook.* Grosset & Dunlap, New York, 1977.

Better Homes and Gardens Christmas-Time Cook Book. Meredith Corp., Des Moines, 1974.

Better Homes and Gardens Homemade Bread Book. Meredith Corp., Des Moines, 1973.

Betty Crocker's Picture Cook Book. McGraw-Hill, New York, 1956.

Blue Ribbon Breads. Country Kitchens Press, Provo, Utah, 1976.

Burton, Katherine and Helmut Ripperberger, *Feast Day Cookbook.* David McKay, New York, 1951.

Cantrell, Rose, *Creative Sourdough Cooking.* Weathervane Books, 1977.

Casella, Dolores, *A World of Breads.* David White Co., New York, 1966.

Claiborne, Craig (ed.), *The New York Times Cook Book.* Harper & Row, New York, 1961.

————, *The New York Times International Cook Book.* Harper & Row, New York, 1971.

Clayton, Jr., Bernard, *The Breads of France,* Bobbs-Merrill, Indianapolis/New York, 1978.

————, *The Complete Book of Breads.* Simon and Schuster, New York, 1973.

The Complete Holiday Cookbook. Favorite Recipes Press, Louisville, Ky., 1969.

David, Elizabeth, *English Bread and Yeast Cookery.* Allen Lane, London, 1978.

Dworkin, Floss and Stan, *Bake Your Own Bread and Be Healthier.* New American Library, New York, 1972.

Fleischmann's Bake-it-easy Yeast Book.

Fleischmann's New Treasury of Yeast Baking.

Food Editors of Farm Journal, *Breads Like Mother Use To Make.* Countryside Press, Philadelphia, 1971.

Goldman, Arnold; Barbara Spiegel; Lyn Stallworth, *The Great Cooks' Guide to Breads.* Random House, New York, 1977.

Gubser, Mary, *Mary's Bread Basket and Soup Kitchen,* William Morrow and Co., Inc., New York, 1975.

Harris, Diane (ed.), *Woman's Day Book of Baking.* Simon and Schuster, New York, 1977.

Harris, Florence La Ganke, *Cooking with a Foreign Flavor.* M. Barrows and Co., Inc., New York, 1952.

The Home Bread Baker. Arco Publishing Co., Inc., New York, 1975.

Honig, Mariana, *Breads of the World.* Chelsea House Publishers, New York, London, 1977.

Marsh, Dorothy B., The Good Housekeeping International Cookbook, Harcourt Brace & World, Inc., New York, 1964.

Nicholls, Nell B. (ed.), Homemade Bread. Doubleday & Co., Inc., Garden City, New York, 1969.

Norman, Ursel, A Basket of Homemade Breads. William Morrow & Co., Inc., New York, 1973.

Pappas, Lou Seibert, Bread Baking. Nitty Gritty Productions, Concord, Calif., 1975.

Pillsbury's Bake Off Breads Cook Book. Pillsbury's Publications, 1968.

Scheer, Cynthia, Mexican Cooking. Owlswood Prods., San Francisco, 1978.

Standard, Stella, Our Daily Bread. Bonanza Books, New York, 1970.

Sturges, Lena E., Breads Cookbook. Oxmoor House, Birmingham, Ala., 1976.

Sunset Books and Sunset Magazine, Editors of, Sunset Book of Breads. Lane Publishing Co., Menlo Park, Calif., 1977.

Tarr, Yvonne Young, The New York Times Bread & Soup Cookbook. Ballantine Books, New York, 1972.

Time-Life Books, Breads. Time-Life Books, Alexandria, Va., 1981.

————, The Time-Life Holiday Cookbook. Time-Life Books, Alexandria, Va., 1976.

Vaughan, Beatrice, *Yankee Hill-Country Cooking.* Gramercy Pub. Co., Los Angeles, 1968.

Voth, Norma Jost, *Festive Breads of Easter.* Herald Press, Scottsdale, Pa., 1980.

Walker, Lorna and Joyce Hughes, *The Complete Bread Book.* Crescent Books, New York, 1977.

Watts, Franklin, *The Complete Christmas Book.* Franklin Watts, Inc., New York, 1961.

Woltner, Annette and Christian Teubner, *Best of Baking.* HP Books, Tucson, Ariz., 1980.

Index